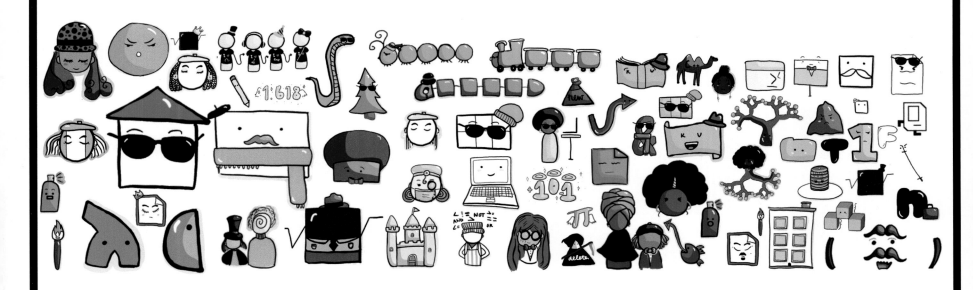

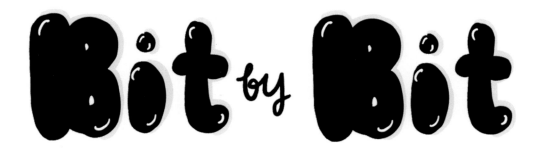

Bit by Bit

A GRAPHIC INTRODUCTION TO COMPUTER SCIENCE

Ecy Femi King

Stanford University Press
Stanford, California

Stanford University Press
Stanford, California

Printed in the United States of America on acid-free, archival-quality paper.

Cataloging-in-Publication Data available upon request.
Library of Congress Control Number: 2024934092
ISBN: 9781503638761 (paper)

Thanks to all those who helped make this project possible!

Sponsor
Stanford VPUE
Undergraduate Major Grant

My Mentors
Lecturer Christina Wodtke
Professor Ge Wang

Summer CS106 Lecturers
Chris Gregg
Jenny Han
Kylie Jue

Friends and Family
Daniel Newton
Juan Espinal-Mejía
Roxane Somda
My Mommy and Daddy ♥
Nina and Rod King

Lucía Morris
Smiti Mittal
Sehajleen Kaur

Stanford University Press
Adam Schnitzer
Alan Harvey

Michele Wetherbee
David Zielonka

Bridget Kinsella
Lizzie Haroldsen

Kendra Schynert

CS Support
Cynthia Lee
Debby Inenaga
James Landay
Jerry Cain
Jim Shea
John Mitchell
And the broader CS and
CS198 Communities

Julie Zelenski
Keith Schwarz
Mehran Sahami
Meredith Hutchin
Nick Troccoli
Ruth Starkman

d.school Support
Glenn Fajardo
Hannah Joy
Aleta Hayes

My Oxford Tutor
Annette Riziki

My UAD
Chad O. Coates

CS106 Alumni
Funmi Solano
Godsfavour Simon
Jack Bartley
Om Jahagirdar

Uche Ochuba
Ulo Freitas
Uma Dayal

CS198 Reviewers
Deveshi Buch
Neel Kishnani
Sam Spinner

Parthiv Krishna
Ricky Parada

Summer CS106A and CS106B Students
Caroline Knoke
Cristian Soler
Diana Vins
Emma Costa
Justin Ho
Nathaniel Mapaye
Venus Nguyen

Aylin Ozdemir
Eric Y. Wang
Erik Vank
Fatima Alhosani
Ismail Syed
Jazmin Can
Joseph Kaim
Julian Bauer

Kanan Aliyev
Paul Sun He
Ranam Hamoud
Shreya Pandey
Shuzi Gong
Stan Stickney
Ziyuan Wang

All those who inspired, supported, and helped me in one way or another :)!

About

"Bit by Bit" is an educational comic exploring the curricula for two of Stanford's most popular courses, the introductory computer science classes CS106A and CS106B.

It is over 160 pages long, many of which are presented through the Fractal Gridding medium. Through colorful characters that personify concepts, storytelling, visual thinking, and the more than occasional pun, Bit by Bit aims to be an unconventional source of both education and entertainment for Stanford students and educators alike. This is the first edition!

The process of creating Bit by Bit was an adventure in art, education, learning, fun, and community collaboration. Each page represents a labor of love. With custom-drawn characters, fun graphics, and original content, it aims to use the power of creativity, art, and visual thinking to supplement potentially intimidating concepts in a friendly way. The content is based upon that of the Summer 2022 version of CS106A and CS106B.

This project was not done in isolation. It involved weekly feedback sessions with students and section leaders of the CS106A and CS106B courses, sage advice from mentors, and the cooperation of lecturers. This led to a network of people from all around the world who helped the Bit by Bit project to thrive. As a section leader for the introductory computer science courses, I witnessed an amazing process of people bonding over the joys of learning CS in a fun way. As a Symbolic Systems major, this project served a grand synthesis of concepts covered in my degree as well as extracurriculars, namely, visual thinking, design, learning psychology, and CS education.

Bit by Bit started as a Stanford VPUE Major Grant Project in Summer 2022.
More information on the book journey can be found on the project website on the right.

How to read the comic

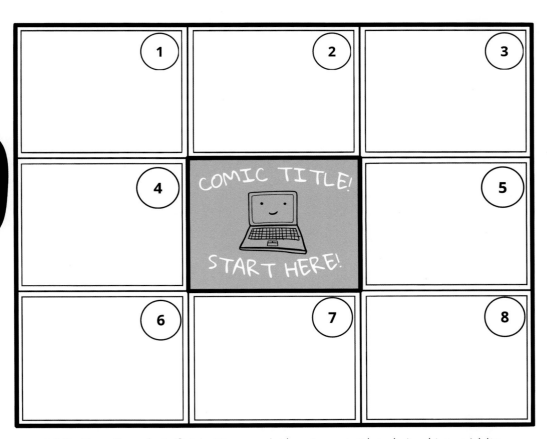

This is a Fractal Grid. To read it, always start in the middle. Afterward, starting from the top row, go from left to right and then do the same for the middle and bottom rows.

WELCOME TO CS106A
Programming Methodology

Welcome to the world of code. We hope you will enjoy your stay—and maybe even extend it!

1. RUN WITH THE PROGRAM

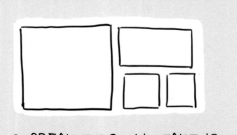
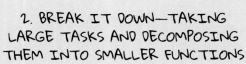

2. BREAK IT DOWN—TAKING LARGE TASKS AND DECOMPOSING THEM INTO SMALLER FUNCTIONS

3. GIVE THE COMPUTER INSTRUCTIONS LINE BY LINE

4. "CELEBRATE THE STRUGGLE"

HERE, WE....

5. TRY TO HAVE PATIENCE AND GROW

6. AIM FOR GOOD STYLE, NOT JUST PERFECT FUNCTIONALITY

7. VALUE CREATIVITY

8. EXPERIMENT WITH THE CODE

CS106A

Fractal Grid of
Contents

Chapter One
THE FUNDAMENTALS

Variable

The Wholly Ints

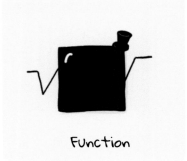

Function

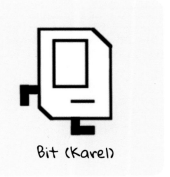

Bit (Karel)

Program

Dr.Err

Variables like VARIABLE temporarily "house" a value. Thus, they are incredibly hospitable!

Welcome to my house! You're welcome to stay as long as you're the right type ;)!

To use a variable, we must first CREATE and then ASSIGN it. We first CREATE a name and then ASSIGN a value using the "=" or assignment operator.

`x = 5`

Welcome to the world x. You are now housing 5.

Howdy! Welcome to my humble abode value 5! Hope you'll enjoy your stay.

This allows us to refer to values such as 5 by a name such as x.

Anywhere I go, I'm now perceived as 5!

`print(x)  # this prints out 5`

Think of the "=" operator as saying "I assign the variable on the left to the right's value."

You can also think of it as saying....
- x now houses 5
- x now is 5
- x evaluates to 5

Meet VARIABLE
A coding classic

AFTER we've given VARIABLE a value, we can REASSIGN the variable, giving it a new value.

Welcome to my house 6 ;)!

bye I guess ;)

```
x = 5
x = 6
print(x)  # this prints out 6
```

We can name our variable pretty much anything we want as long as it is consistent. Since we aim to have good style, it's good to be descriptive with our chosen name.

In this case, my_num looks pretty appealing.

As with everything though, there are a few exceptions. Because variables are names, there are a few things we can't name it.

Don't name me like that!

```
5 = x
 ^
SyntaxError: cannot assign to literal
```

For example, we can't do 5 = x, because 5 is not a name. It is something called a literal. We can put letters then numbers like num5 but can't to the opposite like with 5num.

We use a style called snake case to name variables like VARIABLE.

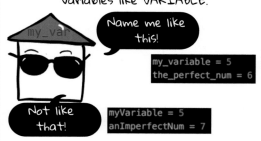

Name me like this!

```
my_variable = 5
the_perfect_num = 6
```

Not like that!

```
myVariable = 5
anImperfectNum = 7
```

hisses

Remember variables from algebra? Here in computing, VARIABLE is VERY SIMILAR. Just like how x in x + y can represent any number in math, variable x can virtually represent any value.

Remember this, kids!

VARIABLE is merely a placeholder waiting to be assigned and reassigned values. By saying x = 5, we are saying x is now 5 and going along with that until we or the code says otherwise.

Howdy, 5! You're welcome to stay as long as the computer says!

So after assigning 5 to x, can x be something that is not a number? Although we technically can, we will want to AVOID that.

I've seen so many different numbers throughout the years... And yet, all of these have been just my type ;)

Variables have something called a TYPE. We want to stick to this type. If variable x has a thing for numbers, only feed it numbers. Don't reassign it to a bunch of letters!

Technically, you can do this, but it feels so so wrong! And can result in confusing code!

```
x = 5
print(x)
x = "howdy!"
print(x)
```

"howdy!"

Meet VARIABLE
A coding classic continued

Sometimes, one variable is set to the value of another. What does this mean? Simply put, the variable on the left now houses the right variable's VALUE.

```
x = 5
y = x   # what's happening here?
```

I assign the variable on the left (y) to the right's value. And what's the value of x? It's 5. So y is now 5.

Remember that the item on the left is always the variable when we assign or reassign. So, it is the one that changes value.

To myself, I am x, but the outer world only sees me as 5 D-: or whatever's in my house. WHYYY???

y = x

Before you use a variable, make sure it exists. Otherwise, the computer will get really mad.

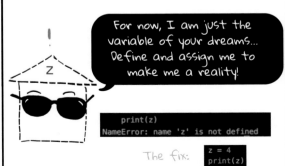

For now, I am just the variable of your dreams... Define and assign me to make me a reality!

```
print(z)
NameError: name 'z' is not defined
```

The fix:
```
z = 4
print(z)
```

As we've seen with print, we can pass variables into functions. We'll see more of this very soon with our friend FUNCTION!

TANGENT: VARIABLES, AN ADDITIONAL REFERENCE

In Python, variables are actually POINTING to a value rather than housing them directly. What does this mean? Variables have a designated SPACE in MEMORY you can think of as their home. This home doesn't actually house the value (like 5) directly but rather gives instructions on how to get to that value.

VARIABLE (instructing computer): Go to address 0x123 to get my value!
COMPUTER: Okay, so you refer to 5. Got it! Thanks!

More specifically, a variable actually hosts the memory ADDRESS of that value. Using this address, Python can then retrieve the actual value.

When we reassign a variable's value, rather than house this new value, the variable actually points to a different value and houses that new memory address.

This information is COMPLETELY IRRELEVANT to actually understand the class. It is for accuracy's sake that I've included it.

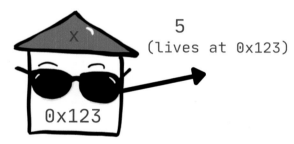

5
(lives at 0x123)

(lives at 0x456)
A more accurate, but less abstracted depiction of variable.

For the purposes of this class, we'll be using the housing analogy, but keep in mind that rather than "housing" a value, the most accurate terminology would be that a variable REFERS to a value or a variable EVALUATES to a value.

Don't expect to understand ANY of this right now. Some of it is covered at the end of CS106B; LOTS and LOTS more is discussed in CS107. It's way beyond the scope of CS106A!

Meet the Wholly Ints. These numbers only include integers, aka WHOLE numbers, be they negative, positive, or zero.

No un-wholly numbers allowed!

After we store the Wholly Ints in a variable, we have a few things we can do with them.

You've seen me before.

`x = 1`

Often, we'll want to add on to a previous value of x. To do this, we can do the following:

`x = x + 5`

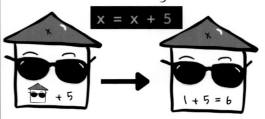

Remember, we are just changing variable x to its previous value plus 5.

Since we often add on to the previous value of x, a shorthand exists that looks like this:

I've appreciated!

```
x += 1 #shorthand
# for x = x + 1
```

My old value + some more value

"x +=" is the same as "x = x +"

The Wholly Ints
They take pride in how wholesome all of them are. And some are simply so natural too!

You may have seen the syntax "++" to add one to an integer. This is NOT allowed in Python.

`x++`

You can't do that to me... At least, not here...

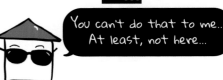

HAHAHAHAHA! Take CS106B to find out more! They have to get through me firsssst

Similarly to addition, we can use this shorthand for subtraction and multiplication.

I've depreciated!   `x -= 3`

And now I've multiplied!!!   `x *= 4`

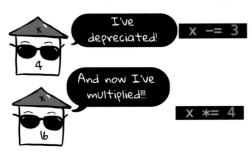

Remember that with the += notation, we are just adding another value to x!

```
y = 2
x += 5
x += y
x += x   # same as x = 2*x
```

Now I'm double the trouble!

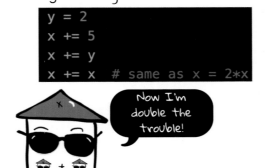

What about division? We'll talk about this later when we talk about floats! For now, don't worry about it, you need not use it!

`x /= 3`

I'm no longer whole D-;

You are no longer a WHOLLY INT. What a pity...

Functions like FUNCTION are black boxes that can do nearly anything! They all have a main GOAL that they pursue.

Function is handed in an INPUT.

And returns to us an OUTPUT called a return value.

performs magic

Some functions are already built into Python.

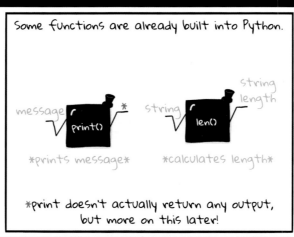

message
print()
string
len()
string length

prints message   *calculates length*

*print doesn't actually return any output, but more on this later!

Other functions we must define for ourselves with the def keyword.

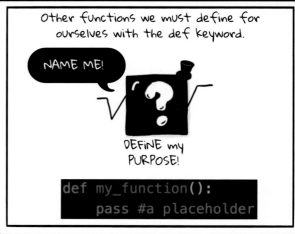

NAME ME!

DEFINE my PURPOSE!

```
def my_function():
    pass #a placeholder
```

We can choose almost any name for our function as long as we are consistent with it.

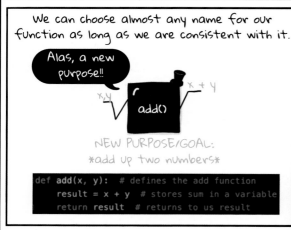

Alas, a new purpose!!

x, y
add()
x + y

NEW PURPOSE/GOAL:
add up two numbers

```
def add(x, y):  # defines the add function
    result = x + y # stores sum in a variable
    return result # returns to us result
```

Meet FUNCTION
A fabulous, fundamental element of our programming adventures

Once we define a function, we can now call it. To do this, we put in OUR OWN input values.

CALL ME BY MY NAME!

(2, 3)
add()
5

```
add(2, 3)  # this returns 5
```

After calling Function, we can then grab its OUTPUT (the return value) by storing it in our old friend variable. VARIABLE can house the RETURN VALUE of any function.

```
x = add(2, 3)
```

Here ya go!

(2, 3)
add()
5

Thanks!

x
5

Make sure a function exists before calling it! I.e., make sure it is built-in or defined by you.

Don't forget to def me as I don't yet exist!!

(3, 2)
subtract()

```
subtract(3, 2)
```

```
    subtract(3, 2)
NameError: name 'subtract' is not defined
```

How do we know when FUNCTION is done? Either we hit a return statement or all the lines finish executing, whichever comes first.

Once I return, I'm DONE!

```
return
```

Since RETURN is the END, even if we write lines after the return, they won't execute.

You might notice that when we defined FUNCTION, we put x & y, but when we called it, we put 2 & 3!

I breathe to you new life

```
def add(x, y):  # defines the add function
    result = x + y  # stores sum in a variable
    return result  # returns to us result
```

Hey Function, we need your help!

```
add(2, 3)  # this returns 5
```

When we DEFINE a function, we also DEFINE our INPUTS with VARIABLES like x and y. These inputs, called PARAMETERS, define how future inputs interact with the function.

Now we're just waiting to get called...

When will some integer come and show up...

Since we are DEFINING our parameters, we can change their names. We just need to ensure that they are consistent within the function.

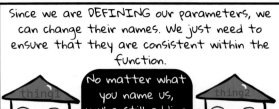

No matter what you name us, you're still adding us together.

```
def add(thing1, thing2):
    result = thing1 + thing2
    return result
```

Descriptive names are best, however! Although we could name our variables tweedle_dee and tweedle_dum or Jollof and stew, names like num1 and num2 are best for readability!

Descriptive enough for ya yet?

Meet FUNCTION
More about parameters

When we CALL a function, we pass SPECIFIC VALUES. These are called ARGUMENTS.

```
add(2, 3)
```

Now we house 2 & 3, sweet!

Since we PASS IN the ARGUMENTS, they must align with the parameters in number and type.

Hey function, can you take in my arguments...

nope, nope, nope, nope

```
add(2) # too few arguments
add(2, 3, 4) # too many arguments
add(3, "hi") # wrong type of argument
add() # too few arguments
```

Arguments can also be variables and functions that evaluate and return the right type.

```
add(add(2, 3), add(4, 5))
```

```
add(5, 9)  # the same thing
```

add(2,3)   add(4,5)

Parameters are super useful for letting us generalize functions!

```
add(1000000000, 10)
add(4, -5)
add(add(10, 10), 50)
```

1000000010
-1
70

add()

Return, return, return! Isn't this like MAGIC?

Panel 1
Let's look at FUNCTION'S OUTPUT, aka its return value, a little bit more!

Panel 2
The return value is a SINGLE VALUE. Recall that VALUES can also be housed by variables.

```
x = add(2,3)
```

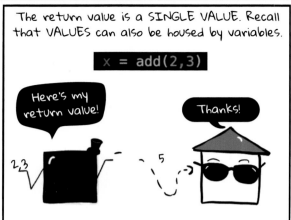

Panel 3
SIDE NOTE: the return value is also of a certain type (a whole number or integer, a string like "hello", etc).

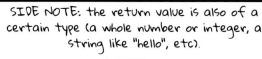

We won't worry too much about that now, however (laughs in C++).

Panel 4
In some cases, FUNCTION doesn't return anything; it returns nothing. In Python, this is actually represented by the value None.

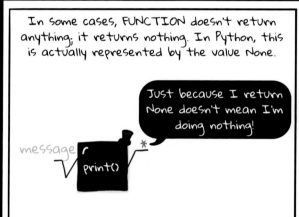

Panel 5
Fabulous FUNCTION
More about return values

Panel 6
In other cases, FUNCTION has no input or output. What do these functions do? Think of functions like bit.move() or a function that prints hello. They still perform a task.

```python
def print_hello():
    print("Hello!")
```

still performs magic

Panel 7
So what's the difference between print and return?

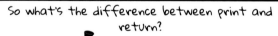

```
print(x)
```
```
return x
```

print(x)	return x
# is its own function	# is a keyword
# when called, the function continues	# immediately ENDS the function
# we see and can read output on screen	# stores value internally
# print function returns nothing	# value can be stored in variable

Panel 8
We would use each when we want to...

```
print(x)
```
```
return x
```

print(x)	return x
# visualize the output	# modify an input
# read out different function parts	# end the function's task
# see and read the output on screen	# pass the output to other functions
# print lines	# store values
# debug	# decompose

Panel 9
CHALLENGE: what would my_var evaluate to? Hint: it's not 3!

```
my_var = print(3)
```

```
my_var = print(3)
Function 'print' doesn't return anything
```

Even Python is trying to warn you here! With print, my_var will (unexpectedly) be None!

Panel 1

~~Sometimes~~ Often, functions call on other functions to help them.

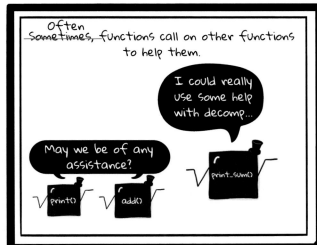

"I could really use some help with decomp..."

"May we be of any assistance?"

print()   add()   print_sum()

Panel 2

Here's an example:

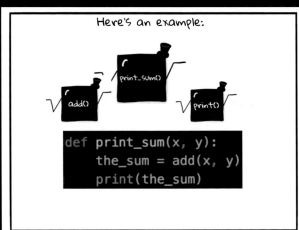

add()   print_sum()   print()

```
def print_sum(x, y):
    the_sum = add(x, y)
    print(the_sum)
```

Panel 3

Helper functions can help us reduce, reuse, and recycle code, helping with decomposition and style :) .

Without decomp	With decomp
`def do_a_360(filename):`	`def do_a_360(filename):`
`    bit = Bit(filename)`	`    bit = Bit(filename)`
`    bit.right()`	`    turn_around(bit)`
`    bit.right()`	`    turn_around(bit)`
`    bit.right()`	
`    bit.right()`	`def turn_around(bit):`
	`    bit.right()`
	`    bit.right()`

This function does a 360° on Bit. Why? Because it looks cool.

Panel 4

Note that the same parameter and variable NAMES don't carry outside of their definition. This is because of something called scope.

"FYI: the_sum only exists in YOUR box!"

print_sum()   add()

Panel 5 (center)

Fabulous FUNCTION
Some more essentials & tidbits

Panel 6

Functions are black boxes that have no other knowledge of what's inside of other functions.

When we call helper functions we can store the return value in our own variable, though.

Panel 7

Some programming OBJECTS like Bit already come with a predefined package of functions. We reference these functions with noun.verb() syntax like bit.move().

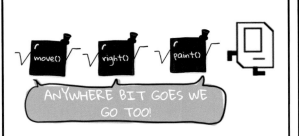

move()   right()   paint()

ANYWHERE BIT GOES WE GO TOO!

Panel 8

So... what makes a BAD function?

"I feeeeel mehhh):"

```
# too long
# unclear what it is doing from looking at it
# does too many tasks WITHOUT decomp
# NO commenting!
# name is unconventional and irrelevant
```

Panel 9

So... what makes a good function?

"I feeeeel goood :)"

```
# has a single job/task
# well-defined and uses helper functions
# breaks down big tasks into smaller ones
# nice commenting!
# name is descriptive and in snake case
```

A Tale of Failed FUNCTIONs

Sometimes, functions just don't work out like how we want them to.

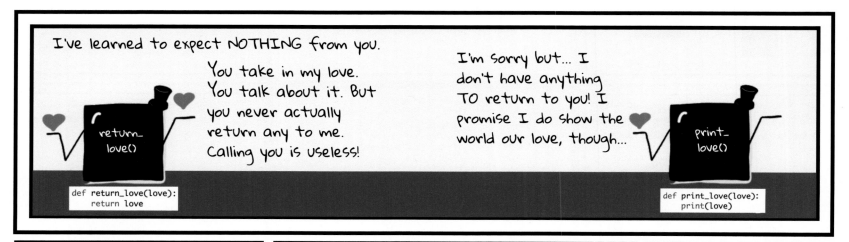

ANATOMY OF BIT
well, bits and pieces of it

How to bring a bit into the world.

bit = Bit(filename)

This is done for us and happens just once! After that, we can pass the bit around in our custom functions.

Suitcase of some Bit Functions
bit.move()
bit.front_clear()
bit.left_clear()
bit.right()
bit.left()
bit.paint(color)

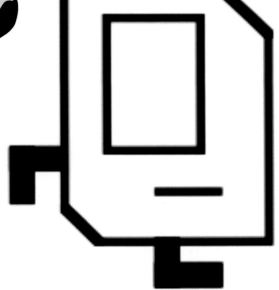

Turn the bit around!
bit.left()
bit.left()

I can see clearly now the wall is gone...
if bit.front_clear() == True:

CANONICAL code: keep on moving forward until you hit a wall

while bit.front_clear():
        move()

Canonical, or idiomatic, code is code used so frequently it's the go-to for when you want to perform a task.

Bit is an object that comes with a bunch of prepackaged functions (sometimes called methods). For these prepackaged functions, we can call them in the noun.verb() format such as bit.predefined_function() as in bit.move() or bit.front_clear(). This is in contrast to functions that we make which get called with the my_function(bit) format, like turn_right(bit). Bit is from the experimental server, made by Nick Parlante!

Scan the QR for more on Bit!

Technically, Bit looks something like this...

1

One day at LaIR...

1

Hey, Program, what do you do?

RUN.

If you look really closely, Program is made up of several functions, all called from one function called Main, but we won't worry about her for now...

Print is in a relationship with the terminal and could never give a return value to function.

I've got eyes for no one else but Terminal. I tell everything to the user that comes my way...

The Booleans are an old married couple who are complete opposites. True and False. I guess opposites really do attract.

A Boolean is anything that evaluates to True or False. More on them is covered in chapter two.

Pycharm Terminal

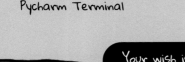

Your wish is your command...

Contains the command line where we run the code and can see print statements.

Additional Friends

Meet some other programming fundamentals, tools, & resources!

Pycharm- a charming IDE indeed integrated development environment

This is the main software you'll use to code your projects.

LaIR, OH, Ed, emails, and your SL!

We're all here to help! For more on resources, go to cs106a.stanford.edu!

Here's a very helpful Python Guide to many class topics.

Pseudocode is a helpful strategy to write good code. Before you start actually coding, you write "fake code" that helps to establish the steps and conceptual flow. Then you can translate this pseudocode into code directly.

3

Often, our code doesn't do what we want it to do! So Dr.Err is here to help us with that. She issues out an error decree, diagnosing what went wrong and helping us to DEBUG.

Hey there! Let's first look at two categories of error.

Type 1: SYNTAX ERROR

PROGRAM:

Fix me!

YOU:

```
# can't run
# called a SYNTAX
error because of a
"grammar" mistake
# error pops up
```

```
# can't do anything
until error is fixed
# at the mercy of
the programming
mistake
# can view error
```

Type 2: LOGIC ERROR

PROGRAM:

Everything looks good to me!

YOU:

But... you're not doing what I want!

```
# runs just fine
# chillin like a villain
# sees NOTHING
wrong
# no error pops up
```

```
# goal vs output
mismatch
# error in thinking
# unintended
mistake or a
misunderstanding
```

I spy a SYNTAX error.

Oops! An unintentional mistake; a _ is invalid syntax!

```
def add(x, y):
    return x _ y
```

Error Making Adventures!
"To err is human, to machine is not"

I spy a LOGIC error.

The code will run, but it'll do the opposite of what you intended it to do.

```
def add(x, y):
    return x - y
```

I spy a LOGIC error, an off-by-one!

Oops! A logical mistake; you are off by one in what to print!

```
def print_0_to_10():
    for i in range(10):
        print(i)
```

This code skips the 10.

Right now, we'll just have to manually fix our errors, or DEBUG our code, but in the future we'll have characters like Doc Test to help us!

YOU (before LaIR)   YOU (after LaIR)

If you have a Big Fat Bug, feel free to go to LaIR (OH) or make an Ed post! We're all here to help you succeed!

Remember, the error is in your syntax or logic. Finding the error in your human ways is the way to debug!

i don' feel so good

I'm here to help!

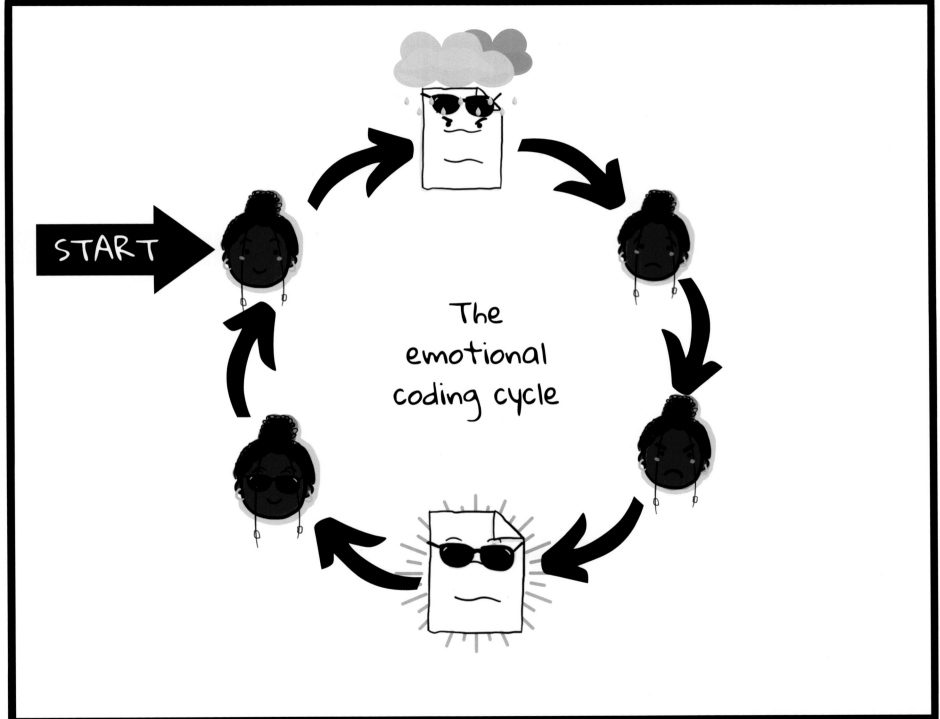

Chapter Two
THE CONTROL FLOW FAMILY AND FRIENDS

The Booleans

The Operator Squad

Mama If Statement

Mr. Infinity Loop

Mr.While

Lady For

Ranger Range

UBNI

The Booleans are true or false values represented by the keywords True and False in Python. The couple's relationship is pretty black and white.

I am the whole truth and nothing but the truth.

Things can truly be False, you know!

The most basic value that evaluates to true is True and the most basic value that evaluates to false is False.

I'm True

And I'm False

If you add the not keyword, it negates the statement, making its value the opposite of what it would have been otherwise.

I'm not False

and I'm not True

The Booleans are often found hanging out with Mama If and Mr. While. The Operator Squad also works under them. We'll meet them on the next page.

The Truth about the Booleans...
Examining some expressions

There are expressions that evaluate to the Booleans. These expressions are called CONDITIONS.

You guys belong with me!

Welcome home!

x = 5

```
x == 5
x <= 10
x >= 5
```

```
x < 3
x == 4
x < -1
```

There is a VERY USEFUL shorthand for when trying to see if something is equal to True.

```
def evaluate(expression):
```
instead of THIS....
```
if expression == True:
    print("a true ex     Expression can be simplified
                          Replace boolean expression with 'expression'
```
you can do THIS....
```
if expression:
    print("a true expression!")
```

Even Pycharm has a preference!

Similarly, there is a VERY USEFUL shorthand for when you're trying to see if something is equal to False.

instead of THIS....
```
if expression == False:
    print("a false expression!")
```
you can do THIS....
```
if not expression:
    print("a false expression!")
```

These two do the exact same thing! One is just MORE code...

The Booleans make for super useful functions where the goal is to figure out yes/no questions.

Is my number prime?

NOPE!

161

False!

isPrime()

figures out if an integer is prime

THE OPERATOR SQUAD

Connecting and conducting expressions since January 1st, 1970

Expressions are bits of code that evaluate to a value! The Operator Squad, working for the Booleans, helps to create expressions that will evaluate to True or False, aka CONDITIONS!

At the Relationship Gates...
In order to give the go to evaluate to true...

Equality	Inequality	Greater Than	Greater Than or Equal	Less Than	Less Than or Equal
Two things need to be the exact same	Two things need to be different	Left > Right	Left >= Right	Left < Right	Left <= Right

These are called relational operators. They tell us whether the relationship between two values is True or False.

At the Logic Gates
In order to give the go to evaluate to true...

De Morgan's law ->
```
!(x and y) = !x or !y
!(x or y) = !x and !y
```

Both sides must be true

At least one side must be true

Makes expressions evaluate to their opposite

NOTE: With the *and* operator, as soon as the left side is False it STOPS. Sometimes this ordering matters.

These are called logical operators. They tell us whether the combination of logical values is True or False.

Not (both sides must be true)

Not (at least one side must be true)

=

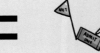

at least one side must be false

=

both sides must be false

9

Once upon a time, there was an ANCIENT statement called Mama If, born of the desire for expression balanced by control.

Despite her name, she was anything but iffy. She could look straight at any condition and evaluate it, seer-like in her perfect accuracy.

> Your condition is True, therefore pass through!

```
def test_condition(condition):
    if condition:
```

Where is the == True? For answers, check out page 18, panels 6 and 7.

In the True condition, the code had the privilege of accessing a special body of knowledge, passed down only once!

> I see your condition is True. Welcome inside to a new body of knowledge! YOLO! You only look once!

```
def test_condition(condition):
    if condition:
        print("knowledge!")
```

Mama If prized her bodies of knowledge, and each one started and ended with indentation to signify their sacredness.

```
if condition:
    print("Special Knowledge!")
    print("as long as you are here...")
    print("your secret is safe!")
    print("but as soon as you exit out of the indent...")
print("no longer special knowledge D-: aka GENERAL knowledge")
    print("can't re-indent D-: once you're out, you're out. ")
```

> Once you leave the world of indentation, you can never go back!

This code will error.

The Control Flow Family: Mama If Statement
Allowing us to conditionally access bodies of knowledge

This introduced some control into the lives of those she touched, allowing bits of code to happen only under specific conditions.

```
if bit.front_clear():
    bit.move()
```

> I want to move, but only if the front is clear!

> Thanks for preventing me from running into a wall!

> Anything for you Bit! I will see if that is true and if so put Bit through.

In the false condition, the code would SKIP the sacred body of knowledge and just go on to the general knowledge.

> Your condition is False. Sorry, no access to the sacred body allowed!

```
def test_condition(condition):
    if condition:
        print("it's true!")
print("For EVERYONE, regardless!")
```

Sometimes, the false condition had its own SEPARATE body of knowledge that everyone ELSE but the true condition could access.

> Your condition is False. Diverting access to another body of knowledge...

```
def test_condition(condition):
    if condition:
        print("it's true!")
    else:
        print("it's false D-:")
```

CHALLENGE: think of a case where two if statements aren't the same as one if-else.

Sometimes there were multiple conditions to check, and then, at the end, a condition for everyone else. These other conditions were contained in elif lines.

```
def legal_to(age):
    if age >= 21:
        print("FULLY LEGAL")
    elif age == 20 or age == 19:
        print("so close to FULLY legal!")
    else:
        print("too young!")
```

> This knowledge for you, that knowledge for you, and something for everyone else!

One day, Ms. If Statement was thrown into a loop after meeting the alluring Mr. Loop. They fell in love over their passion for indentation and subsequently gave birth to Baby While Loop.

Alas, it was True at first sight.

Baby While was a prodigious child who grew up into the noteworthy Mr. While. Like his Mama If, he could evaluate statements on the fly.

Your condition is true...for now... pass through!

`while condition:`

But something was different. The sacred body of knowledge could be accessed multiple times until the condition was no longer true.

Your condition is true...for now. Pass through!
Your condition is true...for now. Pass through!
Your condition is now false! Done!

```
age = 16
while age < 18:
    print("another BIRTHDAY")
    age += 1
print("BOOM! YOU'RE AN ADULT")
```

That's my son!

Mr. While had to do 2 main tasks: evaluate and execute. In the beginning, he evaluated the condition to see if it was true or false.

STEP one: check the condition (evaluation)
STEP two: execute the correct code (execution)

The Control Flow Family: Mr. While Loop
Allowing us to conditionally access bodies of knowledge repeatedly

Next, he executed the appropriate code. In the false condition, he skipped the body of knowledge. In the true one, he read ALL of the sacred body of knowledge WITHOUT STOPPING until all had been read.

ALL or NOTHING, baby!

Even if the condition changed in the middle of the loop, there was no stopping him; he was already set in motion.

After going over EVERY LINE of knowledge, he evaluated the condition once again. If it was true, he went in again; if it was now false, he exited out.

Time to go back up now that I've looked at everything!

It was as if he was a continuous if statement, constantly evaluating and executing until otherwise.

What if Mr. While didn't stop and the condition was always true? Then he'd run into an infinite loop. Uh oh!

```
def be_positive(negative_num):
    while True:
        negative_num += 1
```

I spy a LOGIC error, infinite loop!

Another error! This loop will go on forever and ever!

Feel the wrath of the Loop family!

Sometimes, it was necessary to break out of the while loop completely. This could be done with the BREAK keyword.

```
def be_positive(negative_num):
    while True:
        negative_num += 1
        if negative_num > 0:
            break
```

Are you taking a break from me?

While True and break are sometimes used together as a problem-solving strategy.

Soon, Mama If and Papa Loop had another child—Baby For. Baby For grew up into the exacting and calculating Lady For.

Baby For absolutely admired her older brother While growing up. In her eyes, he could do no wrong. She struggled to feel adequate.

Your balance reminds me of mom.
Your persistence reminds me of dad.
You can do everything and more.
What can't you do?
You're perfect.
What am I even here for?
How can I ever live up to expectations?

But as she grew older, she increasingly became annoyed by his nonchalant attitude.

```
i = 0
num_loops = 5
while i < num_loops:
    print("This prints 5 times")
    i += 1
```

What if I already know how many times to loop through?

But sis... you know I can already do that?

a young For and While

She wondered how she could be more efficient.

But brother, that's so long!

You have no sense of STYLE!

And so...? It gets the job done?

Have you even SEEN me?

The Control Flow Family: Lady For
A new approach to evaluating things

After much soul-searching, Lady For decided to take a slightly different approach to evaluating things than her brother.

`while age < 18:`

`while condition:`   `while True:`

calculates and evaluates

Rather than look at all conditions, she decided to specialize. She only looped through things a predetermined amount of times and actively kept track of that number.

```
for i in range(5):
    pass #does nothing
```

I can loop through automatically, just tell me how many times to execute the body!

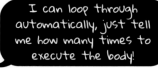

Functionally speaking, her brother COULD do this exactly.

```
i = 0
while i < 5:
    i += 1
```

Just for the record, I can do that too. I can loop through 5 times, easy!

However, her approach took care of some things for us, namely automatically moving through the numbers. This made it so that others needed not keep track!

But that's my specialty, Brother! And I do more work for the user! Just admit it, I've bested you in something!

```
for i in range(5):
    print("This prints 5 times")
```

So how did Lady For accomplish this? She enlisted the help of her built-in partner Range and handy-dandy Variable!

Hey there, the name's Range Function! And I bet you've never met a function LIKE me!

Well, howdy!

Range generated a list of a specified length up to BUT not including that specified number.

`range(5)`

I can give you a list of 5 whole numbers UP TO but not including 5!

More on lists on page 52!

`[0, 1, 2, 3, 4]`

Generates a list of things UBNI the last number

NOTE: In Python 3, you have to do list(range(5))

SIDE NOTE: The concept of UBNI (up to but not including) will pop up a lot! This is because we often start at 0 and then go up to, but don't include the last number.

You may be making 5 numbers, which is 5 items, but 5 never shows up!

`[0, 1, 2, 3, 4]` 5

Lady For would start off the loop and ask for a VARIABLE. Each time through the loop, this variable automatically TRANSFORMED into the next number in range's LIST.

`for i in range(5):`

Creates a variable i that becomes each list item

Generates a list of things to loop through

Technically, we can name the variable anything we want, but i is standard.

The Control Flow Family: Lady For and the Ranger
A legendary friendship

The VARIABLE would AUTOMATICALLY increment for us!

0 1 2 3 4

i AUTOMATICALLY go up for each ITERATION of the loop.

Each time we go through the loop is one iteration.

Range also had a lot of range. There were two optional parameters: the first, a lower bound, the third, the amount to increment by.

```
range(2, 10)
#[2,3,4...9]
```

```
range(2,10,2)
#[2,4,6,8]
```

CHALLENGE: how would we create a list that goes from 0 - 100, counting by tens?

STILL HERE!

In these ways, Lady For was super duper helpful for looping if you knew the EXACT number of times you wanted to do something.

I'm good with numbers!

This could mean doing something a set number of times, counting down, or indexing through something!

If you want to do something 10 times or count down, I'm your gal! Knowing the EXACT number of times to do something for certain is my thing!

3

TALES GROWING UP

As little children, For and While were told lots of stories.

What happens if we don't indent the body of Knowledge inside?

The python snake will actually come after you! LIFE LESSON: Never forget to indent, kids!

A LITTLE ARGUMENT

One day, when Mr. While was still young, he and his Mama If got into an argument. Mama If responded calmly and wisely.

Why do I even need you anymore? I can do everything and more by myself!

I am here to look out for you and help you. You may want to check additional things or check to see if the original condition still holds before you are able to re-evaluate.

He soon realized that they could work together to do great things.

CHALLENGE: Where might we use an if-statement nested in a while loop?

FAMILY DYNAMICS
if only for a little while, family matters!

PERSONALITY DIFFERENCES

- Loves waiting until the right time to do things
- Broad and open-minded
- Can be fast or slow
- Loves the word "until"
- Kind and laidback but also competitive
- Great at handling many unique cases

- Works best under certainty; has difficulty with ambiguity
- Laser-focused
- Constant, steady, and stable
- Loves the word "times"
- Very detail-oriented, intense, and competitive
- Fantastic at her specialty and doing her job

MR. LOOP'S FIRST NAME

Many of you may be wondering what my first name is... It is indeed Infinity! I am Infinity Loop, and often I don't know when to stop. Before I met Mama If, I would always spiral out of control; I was merely existing. She introduced lots of balance into my life. I will forever love and appreciate her for that ;)

"And when we know our strengths and weaknesses, we can function as one big coding family"
- Mama If Statement

Lady For was also very versatile. In addition to going through lists of numbers, she could go through lists of other things.

I love lists because I know the exact number of items in them!

She could even look at each character on a string. Anything with individual elements she could pretty much loop through.

for ch in str
for item in list

I LOVE anything that's indexed!!!

Whereas the for i in range loop was useful for things where the index mattered or numbers mattered or counting down...

I am especially helpful with INDEXING stuff!

the general for each pattern was useful for doing something to each item in a string/list/dict without worrying about the index.

The items in a list

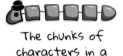

The chunks of characters in a string...

The keys in a dictionary

These characters can be found in ch 4 and 6.

The Control Flow Family: Lady For

Acknowledging Each and Every Item

Differences between the for i in range and more general for each pattern...

`my_list = [1, 2, 3]`

for i in range(len(my_list))	for item in my_list:
• the index matters (e.g., dealing with odd-indexes) • goes through INDEX of items	• we want to do something simple to each element • goes through items

Of course, While could do all of these things, but it felt different. Lady For did so with so much ease and clarity that it was wonderful to watch and witness her style.

I ran so you could walk, Sister

What can I say? I'm in my element.

Generally speaking, differences in when to use the two are when...

• testing out a condition where the number of times we loop through might change
• we're doing something until something else is no longer true

• we know exactly how many times we want to loop through
• we're going through a list, string, etc.

Together, the control flow family did wonders for the coding world.

What BEAUTIFUL children we have!

5

Naturally, there was some sibling rivalry between While and For.

So they went and asked Mama If who was better.

For example, While, you're great for testing out so many different conditions!

Sibling Rivalry:
Lady For vs Mr. While

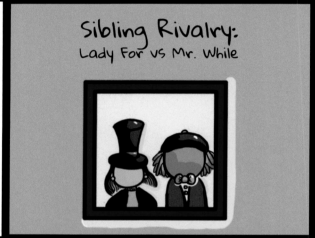

Whereas For, you're the classic go-to for many familiar things.

You both have your unique strengths and differences which should be celebrated!

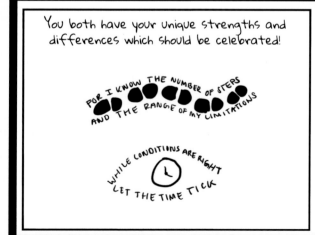

In this world, we all rely on each other, if only for a while...

And when we know our strengths and weaknesses, we can function as one big coding family!

2

GO TO LaIR

When I was but a frosh, taking CS106A in the winter, I had heard tales of LaIR from fall quarter. I thought it was "the lair." As its name would suggest, I envisioned a dark basement, full of computers that people cried in front of while trying to fix their code.

I went a few times over the course of CS106A and B when I was really struggling, and it saved me hours of trying to figure bugs out all by myself!

You too should utilize the amazing community that's here to help you become the best coder possible! LaIR can be found at paperless.stanford.edu with more details on the course website.

Fun fact: LaIR stands for Library and Information Resources. I don't quite remember what that is (or was), but since my time at Stanford, LaIR has been hosted in Tressider, online, and most recently, in Durand.

Chapter Three
A COORDINATED BUNCH
Floats, Pixels, and Grids

The floats

Mr. Pixel

OBO

Syz N

Marge N

Fillip N

Griddy

Sand Griddy

Remember the Wholly Ints? They're great for WHOLE numbers, but how we can represent some other not-so-wholly numbers?

fractions

The irrationals

To represent decimals, we have a type called floating points, or floats.

We are the floats!

With them, we can represent my favorite value of all.... pi!!!!!!

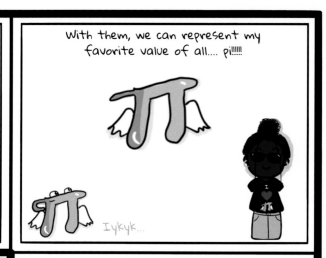

Iykyk...

Float values have a decimal even when they are whole numbers.

You may be a perfect number 6, but I am the perfect 4.0!

literally a perfect number

There are other ways to be perfect too, you know...

Meet the Floats
Doing more than just floating around

So why use ints at all? Since they guarantee a whole number, they are useful for things such as indexing.

You can't go into index 2.5. That's invalid!

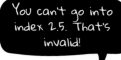

More on lists can be found in chapter 4.

Floats are good for things involving precise numbers and calculations.

What's the exact distance from here to the rocket?

Oh.... I dunno, 10 miles

10.2846 miles, ma'am!

Floats are generally used for things such as...

decimal/general calculations
math formulas
data and scientific analysis
precision/exact things

Sometimes, we need to keep both types separate. But how can we do so when they are so intertwined in our programming world?

We are wholly and grounded, while your head is in the clouds!

Are you sure it's not the other way around?

When we are dividing, there are some interesting things going on with both the Floats and the Wholly Ints.

"Indeed, there is a great divide between us!"

"Really?"

For example, which of these would produce a float and which would produce an int?

$$7.5 / 2.5 = 3 \text{ or } 3.0$$

$$16 / 2 = 8 \text{ or } 8.0$$

$$5 / 2.5 = 2 \text{ or } 2.0$$

The answer is actually a float for ALL of them! In Python, there is int division and float division. Float division is done with the regular division "/" sign.

SIDE NOTE: This was not always the case! Coding is its own language subject to change.

This means that anytime we do float division, or division with the "/", the answer will be followed with a decimal, even if it's whole.

$$7.5 / 2.5 = 3.0$$

$$16 / 2 = 8.0$$

$$5 / 2.5 = 2.0$$

Division between the Wholly Ints and Floats
An unexpected divide

There is also integer division. This is represented by the "//" sign.

Given integer inputs, it yields a whole number that is rounded down. This is also known as floor division.

"Phew! It's back to just being us wholly ints!"

$$16 // 5 = 3$$

What would this be useful for? In some instances, ESPECIALLY with indexing, we have to use an integer when we do math.

What if we want an element that is halfway through a list?

"Well, you can't half index into me!"

More on lists can be found in ch 4

Here are some more differences:

Float Division:	Int Division:
# the default	# calculating indexes
# when exactness matters	# width and height calculations
# when decimals don't matter	# when whole numbers matter

1

This is Mr. Pixel. Despite his initially unassuming aura, he is more brilliant than he first lets on.

He's a very principled person, defined by three main values: R, G, and B. Sometimes, he likes to think they stand for RUGBY. But they stand for Red, Green, and Blue.

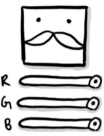

Each one of his RGB values is made up of a number on a scale of 0-255. Mr. Pixel's RGB values can be ramped up or down. 0 is off; 255 is completely on.

With your help, he can change the values, turning certain colors all the way up to full brightness and turning others off.

So, you go to Stanford, huh?

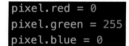

```
pixel.red = 0
pixel.green = 255
pixel.blue = 0
```

Meet Mr. Pixel
Colorfully complex

Grey is a balancing act between all three of the color values.

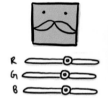

```
pixel.red = 170
pixel.green = 170
pixel.blue = 170
```

You can also combine colors. These colors represent light, and light-mixing (aka additive coloring) may be different than what you might normally expect.

R + G = yellow   G + B = cyan

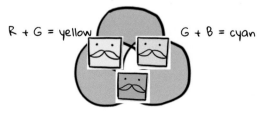

R + B = magenta

With this system, you can essentially make any color and, subsequently, image!

PIXEL PARTY!!!!

Indeed, Mr. Pixel has a very colorful persona.

SATURDAY — So glad to meet you!

SUNDAY — I must admit... I'm feelin' a little blue

MONDAY — GRRR...

3

TANGENT: HOW TO HEX A DECIMAL
Bewitching numbers into Base 16.

If you've ever seen some mysterious scrawl like #8C1515 or #FFFFFF and are curious, this is the spell for you!

So far, we've seen the RGB values on a scale from 0 - 255. Very often, they are actually represented by three two-digit values such as 8C, 15, and 15, as in #8C1515. Each of these secretly represents the three RGB values we know as 141, 21, 21.

#8C1515

Together they make a pretty tree-rific color! It just so happens that 8C, 15, and 15 are the decimal values 141, 21, and 21 in hexadecimal.

Go Card!

R ⊖────●────
G ⊖──●───────
B ⊖─●────────

pixel.red = 141
pixel.green = 21
pixel.blue = 21

Hexadecimal is like our number system, but instead of being based on ten, it is based on sixteen. We also have some "new" numbers. The letter A represents ten, B eleven, up to F, fifteen.

In HEX, the numbers 0 - 16 look like this:

00 01 02 03
04 05 06 07
08 09 0A 0B
0C 0D 0E 0F
10

The rightmost decimal place is the number of ones; the left of that is the number of sixteens. For example, 10 = 0 ones + 1 sixteen = 16.

In other words, instead of each position indicating how many tens there are, it indicates how many sixteens.

16-32 look like this...

10 11 12 13
14 15 16 17
18 19 1A 1B
1C 1D 1E 1F
20

and 240-255 look like this...

F0 F1 F2 F3
F4 F5 F6 F7
F8 F9 FA FB
FC FD FE FF

This 2-digit color format is shorter and more readable!

Hope you enjoyed our little spell lesson!

#8C1515

Sometimes, Mr. Pixel aspires to be more like his good friend Pixie Pixel. So he copies her values.

Sure!

My, my, what beautiful colors you have. May I...?

We can do this by setting Mr. Pixel's RGB values to Pixie Pixel's RGB values.

Thanks! Now we're the same color.

```
pixel.red = pixie_pixel.red
pixel.green = pixie_pixel.green
pixel.blue = pixie_pixel.blue
```

Mr. Pixel has PREPACKAGED ATTRIBUTES in addition to prepackaged functions like bit.move() and bit.left(). For Mr. Pixel, these are his R, G, and B values.

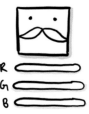

R
G
B

By default, Mr. Pixel and the other image pixels are white when we first create the image.

We can edit Mr. Pixel's prepackaged characteristics once we have access to him. But the question becomes: how DO we GET access to Mr. Pixel and other pixel objects?

How DO you get ahold of me?

Mr. Pixel's Home
Surprisingly colorful

It turns out that Mr. Pixel and all the other pixels live in the underground Image Apartment complex called "The Image".

THE IMAGE APARTMENT COMPLEX

We can access an EXISTING image and store it in a variable by doing the following:

I am now all opened up and ready to use!

```
the_image = SimpleImage(filename)
```

This opens up an image file as a list of each row. This is usually done for us, though.

Filename is a variable that will usually be something like 'main_quad.jpg'.

In the_image, every Pixel has its own apartment coordinate.

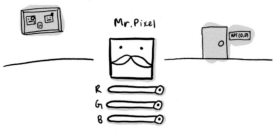

Mr.Pixel

R
G
B

APT (0,0)

Mr. P lives at apartment coordinate (0,0).

Once we have the building and a pixel's apartment coord, we can access it with the syntax the_image.get_pixel(x, y). The function will return to us the pixel object.

```
the_image = SimpleImage(filename)
# to retrieve a specific pixel
mr_pixel = the_image.get_pixel(0, 0)
```

We can store Mr. Pixel in a variable and then edit him as normal, yay!

The Image apartment complex has a certain width and height, represented by the window width and floor height. We can access these values the following way:

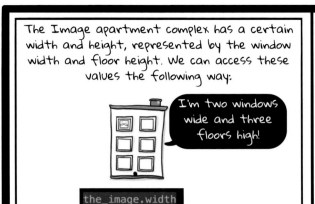

I'm two windows wide and three floors high!

`the_image.width`
`the_image.height`

This image building is also underground, however. It GROWS from the TOP LEFT to the BOTTOM RIGHT.

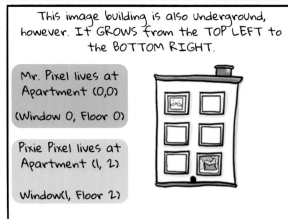

Mr. Pixel lives at Apartment (0,0)
(Window 0, Floor 0)

Pixie Pixel lives at Apartment (1, 2)
Window(1, Floor 2)

The x values grow from left to right as one might expect...

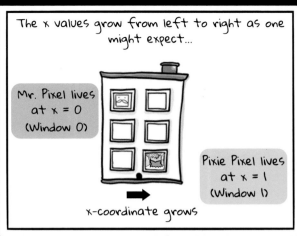

Mr. Pixel lives at x = 0
(Window 0)

Pixie Pixel lives at x = 1
(Window 1)

x-coordinate grows

However, the y values at the top are 0, and the ones at the bottom are the highest.

Mr. Pixel lives at y = 0
(Floor 0)

Pixie Pixel lives at y = 2
(Floor 2)

y-coordinate grows

This is a different set up than in math.

Mr. Pixel's Home
Examining the Underground image complex

Notice that the building is also zero-indexed, meaning that the starting COORDINATE is (0,0).

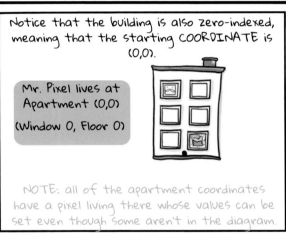

Mr. Pixel lives at Apartment (0,0)
(Window 0, Floor 0)

NOTE: all of the apartment coordinates have a pixel living there whose values can be set even though some aren't in the diagram.

The maximum width and height COORDINATES are image.width - 1 and image.height - 1 though. So the bottom right coordinate is (image.width - 1, image.height - 1).

Even though the building has a width of 2 and height of 3, Pixie Pixel, who lives at the maximum width and height, lives at (1, 2).

These calculations with width and height are often subject to off-by-one errors.

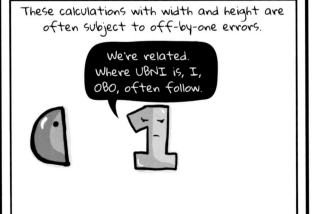

We're related. Where UBNI is, I, OBO, often follow.

As a general rule, when dealing with COORDINATES, you'll have to deal with this zero-indexing, as opposed to sizing.

Accessing one of our coordinates? Remember that we're zero-indexed!

5

So what if we want to modify every pixel in The Image building? Say we want to halve each pixel's RGB's values to save light?

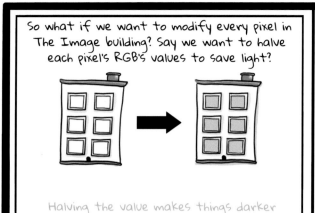

Halving the value makes things darker because we are subtracting light.

We know once we get a pixel like Mr. Pixel, we can do the following code to halve the red value. We can then do this to the G and B values.

```
# halves the red value
mr_pixel.red = mr_pixel.red/2
```

We can do mr_pixel.red /= 2 instead!

But how do we get ACCESS to EVERY pixel coordinate and eventually store each pixel in a variable and update its values?

How are you going to get us pixels in the first place?

We can loop through the building! We can start by visiting each floor number, but that doesn't get us each tenant's coordinate.

```
for floor in range(the_image.height):
```

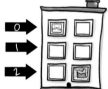

We go through 0, 1, 2, which represent the floor number/ y-coordinate.

```
for y in range(the_image.height):
```

We are looping through each y COORDINATE.

Mr. Pixel's Home
Modifying the current building

But once we have a floor number, we can loop through every window. This does allow us to hit every tenant!

```
for floor in range(the_image.height):
    for window in range(the_image.width):
```

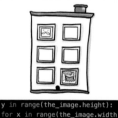

We go through on floor 0: window 0, window 1, on floor 1: window 0, window 1 on floor 2: window 0, window 1.

```
for y in range(the_image.height):
    for x in range(the_image.width):
```

This NESTED for-loop structure allows us to grab every floor/window combination by getting each x, y apartment coordinate.

```
for y in range(the_image.height):
    for x in range(the_image.width):
        pixel = the_image.get_pixel(x, y)
        pixel.red /= 2 # halves the pixel
```

When y is 0, we go through...
x as 0, 1
when y is 1, we go through...
x as 0, 1
when y is 2, we go through...
x as 0, 1.

Once we have a pixel's coordinate, we can access the pixel itself and change it. As the loop grabs every pixel's coordinate, we can modify every pixel!

```
for y in range(the_image.height):
    for x in range(the_image.width):
        pixel = the_image.get_pixel(x, y)
        pixel.red /= 2    # halves the pixel
        pixel.green /= 2  # halves the pixel
        pixel.blue /= 2   # halves the pixel
```

MISSION ACCOMPLISHED!

One common pattern is the following
1) loop through every pixel COORDINATE
2) grab the pixel at the apartment coordinate
3) modify the pixel's RGB values as needed.

```
for y in range(the_image.height):
    for x in range(the_image.width):
        pixel = the_image.get_pixel(x, y)
        # do something with pixel's
        # red, green, blue values
```

Sometimes, we'll want to create a new image building by MODIFYING the design of an old one. This new building is called The Out Image. It has 3 main designers, all with their own artistic visions.

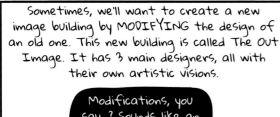

> Modifications, you say...? Sounds like an architectural redesign!

To create this new Out Image building, they start fresh by creating a BLANK building. But how to decide the dimensions? Let's start with those of the previous building.

```
# creates a blank image of custom width and height
the_out_image = SimpleImage.blank(the_image.width, the_image.height)
```

THE IMAGE APARTMENT COMPLEX

THE OUT IMAGE APARTMENT COMPLEX

> You're me, but totally blank!

Often, however, this building will have different dimensions than the original. This is where Syz N's vision comes into play.

> I envision a place with windows twice as wide as The Image! Furthermore, it will be two copies of the original, side by side!

THE IMAGE: THE OUT IMAGE:

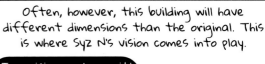 

```
# creates a blank image of custom width and height
the_out_image = SimpleImage.blank(the_image.width*2,
                                  the_image.height)
```

After resizing, we have to figure out how to clone The Image's pixels over. If our goal is to make two copies of the building, how do we clone the right pixels at the right places?

> I have been cloned twice!

The Out Image Architects
Getting to Know Syz N

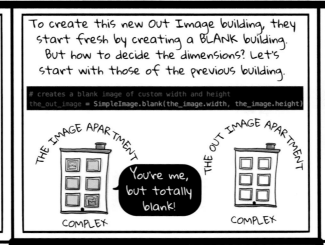

For EACH pixel in The Image, we have to figure out where it is cloned in The Out. In this case, every pixel in The Image is going pop up in two different places.

> In the Image, I'm at 0,0!

> And I will be cloned at (0,0) and (2,0) in The Out!

Cloning involves copying pixel values over.

This involves some calculations.

```
# first, we loop through all The Image's coordinates
for y in range(the_image.height):
    for x in range(the_image.width):
        # grab the pixel from The Image at that coord
        pixel = the_image.get_pixel(x, y)
        # grab The Out first copy pixel
        out_pixel = the_out_image.get(x, y)
        # grab The Out second copy pixel
        out_pixel2 = the_out_image.get(x + the_image.width, y)
        # set the blank pixels in The Out to the one from The Image
        out_pixel.red = pixel.red
        out_pixel2.red = pixel.red
        # and repeat for green and blue
```

THE IMAGE: THE OUT IMAGE:

After the FIRST loop iteration, The Out looks like this!

Syz N really enjoys resizing the building. This involves modifying the dimensions of the Out Image RELATIVE to the Image, whether it be multiplying or adding.

THE OUT IMAGE:

THE IMAGE:

> I envision a place where there are two more sets of floors!

```
the_out_image = SimpleImage.blank(the_image.width,
                                  the_image.height + 2)
```

Indeed, Syz N enjoys her job, and often, she is the first architect called, as resizing is often the first step in creating a new building.

> First and foremost, you'll probably need me!

NOTE: remember to return the_out_image!

Let's next take a look at Marge N. She loves to live on the edge, envisioning worlds in which everything has a little extra margin.

Margins are often added to TWO sides. With a margin m, we would add 2m to the width if we have a left/right margin, and 2m to the height if it's a top/bottom margin.

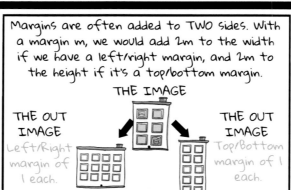

THE IMAGE

THE OUT IMAGE
Left/Right margin of 1 each.

THE OUT IMAGE
Top/Bottom margin of 1 each.

```
the_out = SimpleImage.blank(the_image.width + 2*m, the_image.height)
the_out = SimpleImage.blank(the_image.width, the_image.height + 2*m)
```

Before we enlist the help of Marge N, we often have to consult Syz N. Why? Adding margins adds size to the original image.

I want to add a margin of 1 on the left and right!

I'll add 2 to The Out's width then!

```
# creates a blank image of custom width and height
the_out = SimpleImage.blank(the_image.width + 2,
                            the_image.height)
```

To make her changes, Marge N often has to make use of multiple for loops, including one for JUST The Out and its margins!

I want to make the Pink House! The Image, but with one pixel margins on the left and right!

THE OUT IMAGE
vision

The Out Image Architects
Welcome to the edge with Marge N

The left margin is only applicable to The Out Image. So, we can loop through its x-coordinates in the margin, and then go through all of the y-coordinates as normal.

```
for y in range(the_out.height):
    for x in range(m):
        left_pixel = the_out.get_pixel(x, y)
        left_pixel.red = 255
        left_pixel.green = 0
        left_pixel.blue = 255
```

We can make a blank pixel this shade of pink (magenta) by setting its G value to 0.

Since the right margin is just a shifted left margin, we can get the corresponding pixel in the same loop with some math.

(0,0)
(x, y)

(3,0)
(x + out.width - m, y)

```
right_pixel = the_out.get_pixel(x + the_out.width - m, y)
right_pixel.red = 255
right_pixel.green = 0
right_pixel.blue = 255
```

There are LOTS of ways to do this math.

Combined, the code for the MARGINS looks like this:

```
for y in range(the_out.height):
    for x in range(m):
        left_pixel = the_out.get_pixel(x, y)
        left_pixel.red = 255
        left_pixel.green = 0
        left_pixel.blue = 255

        right_pixel = the_out.get_pixel(x + the_out.width - m, y)
        right_pixel.red = 255
        right_pixel.green = 0
        right_pixel.blue = 255
```

The Pink House is really magenta!

Then, we still have ANOTHER loop over The Image to copy over its pixels to the corresponding ones in The Out image.

```
for y in range(the_image.height):
    for x in range(the_image.width):
        image_pixel = the_image.get_pixel(x, y)
        out_pixel = the_out.get_pixel(x + m, y)
        out_pixel.red = image_pixel.red
        out_pixel.green = image_pixel.green
        out_pixel.blue = image_pixel.blue
```

VISION REALIZED!

NOTE: remember to return the_out!

The work of Fillip N can also be quite involved. He likes to flip buildings either horizontally or vertically.

After my work, you will be welcomed to the flipped side!

Often, Fillip N does not need to consult Syz N. He just likes to experiment with pixel placement and can flip the pixel's POSITIONS.

THE IMAGE   THE OUT IMAGE

Same size with a horizontal flip!

If we are merely flipping, we retain the same dimensions from The Image in The Out. This time around, let's use The LUXURY Image Apartment to illustrate.

```
the_out = SimpleImage.blank(the_image.width, the_image.height)
```

THE LUXURY IMAGE   THE OUT IMAGE
APT COMPLEX   APT COMPLEX

If we are horizontally flipping, that is, flipping along the x-axis, the x-apartment coordinate changes, but not the y. So we need to figure out the math for that!

I'm at (0,0)!

And I'm at (4,0)!

The Out Image Architects
Welcome to the flip side with Fillip N

When Mr. Pixel is at the first x, flipping him takes him to the last x. But when he's ONE from the start, flipping takes him ONE from the end. And when he's TWO from the start, flipping takes him TWO from the end.

I'm one from the start!

I love the middle.

I'm one from the end!

Me too!

So, in The Image, we can grab the pixels from left to right and clone those in The Out from right to left.

```
the_image = SimpleImage(filename)
the_out = SimpleImage.blank(the_image.width, the_image.height)
for y in range(the_image.height):
    for x in range(the_image.width):
        image_pixel = the_image.get_pixel(x, y)
        out_pixel = the_out.get_pixel(the_image.width - 1 - x, y)
        out_pixel.red = image_pixel.red
        out_pixel.green = image_pixel.green
        out_pixel.blue = image_pixel.blue
```

Since we're dealing accessing the last coordinate, we have to grab the_image.width - 1.

The process for vertical swaps is similar. Instead of the x-coordinate, though, the y-coordinate is now the one that's reversed in The Out.

```
out_pixel = the_out.get_pixel(x, the_image.height - 1 - y)
```

I'm at (0,0)!

And I'm at (0,3)!

Drawing and mapping all transformations with the Image Architects is very useful!

DRAW IT OUT! Also check out the QR Code! It's our gift to you for learning about images and pixels!

Meet Griddy! He is a 2D figure that likes to host all kinds of values in his cells. These values are often characters representing objects. Let's make 'b' a bubble and 'r' a rock!

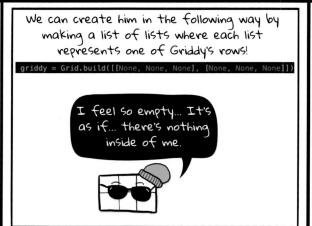

I'm Bubs!

And I, Rock!

```
[[None, None, None], ['b', None, 'r']]
```

We can create him in the following way by making a list of lists where each list represents one of Griddy's rows!

```
griddy = Grid.build([[None, None, None], [None, None, None]])
```

I feel so empty... It's as if... there's nothing inside of me.

The Image and Griddy have a lot more in common than you would initially think...

Not quite.

TWINSIES!!!

Griddy and The Image are both zero-indexed and start from the top left.

To my top left is (0,0)!

Meet Griddy
Hosting the coolest characters on the block

Both Griddy and The Image have a height and width we can access and loop through.

```
for y in range(griddy.height):
    for x in range(griddy.width):
        pass  # do something
```

Loop de doo de loop! La dee da dee da!

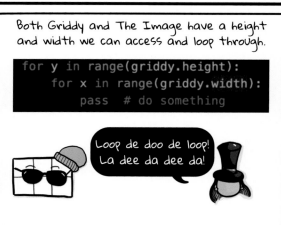

Sometimes, we'll want to loop from the bottom to the top rather than from top to bottom. To do this, we can reverse the order of the y-coordinates like so.

```
for y in reversed(range(griddy.height)):
    for x in range(griddy.width):
        pass  # do something
```

Row 1:
x as 0, 1, 2
Row 0:
x as 0, 1, 2

Grids are often already populated with characters when we deal with them.

You know, I'm also full of depth and character!

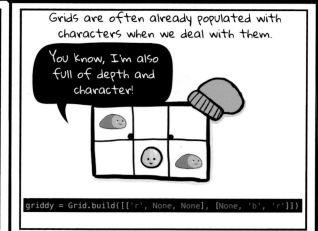

```
griddy = Grid.build([['r', None, None], [None, 'b', 'r']])
```

To access one of Griddy's values, we can use the grid.get() function. For this, we need the (x,y) LOCATION of the value first.

```
for y in range(griddy.height):
    for x in range(griddy.width):
        value = griddy.get(x, y)
        print(value)
```

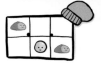

CHALLENGE: What would this print?

Sometimes, the (x, y) location will be given to us. Other times, we'll loop through them. Under the hood, this is value = griddy[y][x].

Sometimes, we'll want to add a character to Griddy. We can do this with the grid.set() function.

```
griddy.set(2, 0, 'b')
```

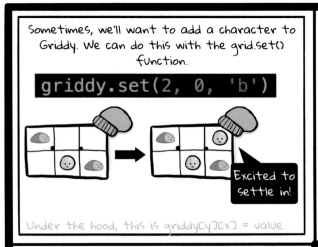

Excited to settle in!

Under the hood, this is griddy[y][x] = value.

Sometimes, we want to MOVE a character from one cell to another. To do this, we GET the character, SET its current location to NONE, and then SET its destination.

```
# moves the bubble at 1,1 to its left coordinate 0, 1
val = griddy.get(1, 1)  # get and store value
griddy.set(1, 1, None)  # clear current location
griddy.set(0, 1, val)  # set destination to value
```

Yay! A new neighbor!

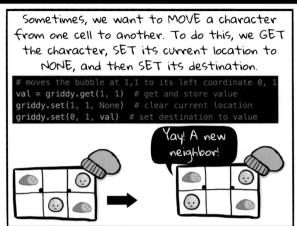

With grids, we'll often want to access values relative to a coordinate. That includes accessing whatever is to the left or right, top or down, and even diagonal to a spot.

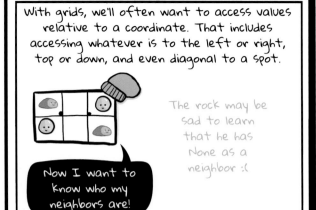

The rock may be sad to learn that he has None as a neighbor :(

Now I want to know who my neighbors are!

Here is a summary of that math.

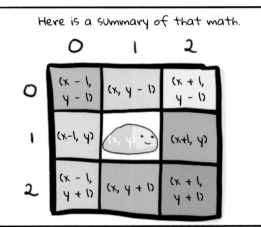

	0	1	2
0	(x − 1, y − 1)	(x, y − 1)	(x + 1, y − 1)
1	(x−1, y)	(x, y)	(x+1, y)
2	(x − 1, y + 1)	(x, y + 1)	(x + 1, y + 1)

Meet Griddy
Looking at the neighbors on the block

Be careful! Some of these coordinates may not be in bounds. If we try to access an out-of-bounds coordinate, Griddy will get MAD. And we don't want to see griddy mad.

```
griddy.set(3, 0, None)
```

What do you think you're doing?

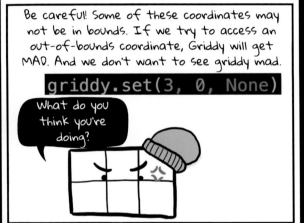

To avoid this, before accessing a coordinate, you should check whether it is in bounds with the grid.in_bounds() function, which returns a Boolean based on if x,y is in bounds.

```
if griddy.in_bounds(x, y):
    value = griddy.get(x, y)
    griddy.set(x, y, None)
    print(value)
```

IF you're in bounds, feel free to continue!

An alternative approach is to immediately return if a condition is violated (one strike and you're out), rather than continue forward if all conditions are met (passing through all the gates of truth).

```
if not griddy.in_bounds(x, y):
    return
value = griddy.get(x, y)
griddy.set(x, y, None)
print(value)
```

If you're not in bounds you can just bounce!

More on Griddy and grids can be found here!

1

Q: Why do coders like to use dark mode?

A: Because bugs are attracted to the light.

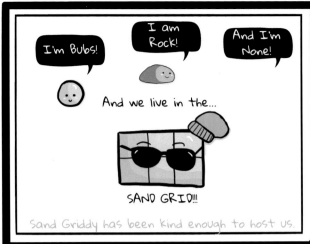

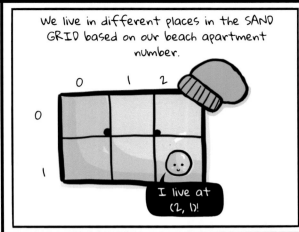

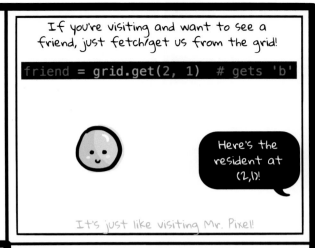

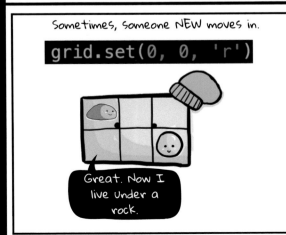

Chapter Four
STRINGS, LISTS, AND LOOSE ENDS

The String Snake

Listy the List Train

Queen Main

Doc Test

File

This is the string snake. It is made up of a bunch of characters STRUNG together.

```
string_snake = 'pi 3?!'
```

Each one of these characters is a value with its own characteristics. It may be a letter, digit, space, or other symbol.

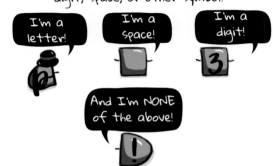

There are various functions that can tell us IF the character is of a certain type. These return True/False.

```
if ch.isalpha():
    print("it's alphabetical!")
elif ch.isdigit():
    print("it's a digit")
else:
    print("it's a surprise!")
```
```
if ch.isupper():
    print("UPPER CASE!")
elif ch.islower():
    print("lower case")
else:
    print("not alpha")
```

In Python, we can use single quotes or double quotes to represent strings and characters.

Double quotes must be used if there's a single quote in the string like an apostrophe.

Meet the String Snake
Stringing together characters of all kinds.

To get an idea of how long he is, aka his length, we can use the len() function.

```
string_snake = 'python'
str_len = len(string_snake)   # is 6
```

An empty string with a length of zero is represented by quotes with NO space in between them.

```
empty_str = ''
```

The string snake is also zero-indexed. Each character has an index, with the FIRST character being at index 0.

Be careful not to index beyond 5 or you will get an error!

Because of this indexing, we can loop through the string snake with a good old friend!

```
# both loops print every character in string
for i in range(len(string_snake)):
    print(string_snake[i])  # uses indexing
for char in string_snake:
    print(ch)  # uses characters directly
```

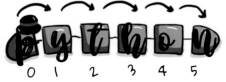

There are also different ways we can combine string snakes. This is called concatenation.

UNITE!

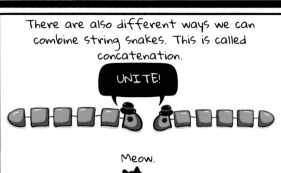

Meow.

We can append one string to another, that is add another string to the end of our string.

Say hello to moi, the new string snake!

```
str_snake = str_snake + '!'
```

Just like adding to integers, we can shorten this notation.

```
str_snake += '!'
```

We can also add another string to the beginning of our string, but can't simplify this notation.

```
#  adds to front
str_snake = '@' + str_snake
```

Meet the String Snake
Some concatenation patterns

The string snake is immutable. That means we can't actually modify the snake itself.

Please don't change me! Recreate me if you will!

We can't change a single character, nor use an erase or append function for the string directly.

```
# not allowed
str_snake[7] = '?'
str_snake.append('?')
```

What do you think you're doing? No appendage FUNCTIONS allowed, nor editing of me directly.

```
TypeError: 'str' object does not support item assignment
```

So, what is s += '!' doing then? We are actually creating a COPY of the snake to replace the original.

```
str_snake = str_snake + '!'
```

In creating me...

you are destroying and overwriting me!

```
str_snake = '@' + str_snake
```

So, when we want to modify a string, we'll often start from an empty string and rebuild.

Get used to seeing s = or s+=. I'll be shedding my skin a lot!

Don't worry if this immutable stuff is a wee bit confusing. Just remember that you can't do something like string[i] = 'a' and that you'll be using s = alot!

We know how to access a single slice, aka index into a string, but what if we want more of the string than just a single character?

```
fourth_char = str_snake[3]
```

We can slice into the string with [:] notation. Let's say we want to get the substring 'py'. We can do the following:

```
py_part = str_snake[1:3]
```

Guess we're NOT PYT material....

NOTE: this goes UBNI the last index.

If we want to get the rest of the string, we start with the index we want, inclusive, and then just omit the last index.

```
rest = str_snake[3:]
```

If we want to get up to but not including an index, we can go UBNI that index, omitting the first index.

```
up_to = str_snake[:3]
```

Once again, index 3 is not included.

Meet the String Snake
String Slicing

Since our string is 0-indexed, the last index is the length of the string - 1.

```
last_char = str_snake[len(str_snake) - 1]
```

GET USED TO SEEING THIS SYNTAX!!!!

PRO TIP: s[-1] also accesses the last index in a nice and succinct way.

```
last_char = str_snake[len(str_snake) - 1]
also_last_char = str_snake[-1]
```

Ooh, a shortcut!

Python allows for backwards indexing where s[-1] gets the last character in a string s and s[-2] gets the second to last.

If we want all of the string, we can just leave the colon there alone.

```
whole_str = str_snake[:]
```

Why someone would do this I'm not entirely sure...

SIDE NOTE: If you index beyond the last index, you'll have an error. But if you are slicing with the colon, there will be none.

```
err = str_snake[20]
no_err = str_snake[1:20]
no_err2 = str_snake[20:40]
no_err3 = str_snake[:20]
no_err4 = str_snake[20:]
```

EXTRA CHALLENGE: what do all the no_err variables evaluate to?

We may see this with parsing and s[begin:end] where end may go beyond.

Sometimes, we want to check if a character is in a string. We can do this with the `in` keyword which gives us a boolean.

```python
if '!' in str_snake:
    print('excitement found!')
```

Hey do you happen to have an exclamation?

That is True!

We can also check if something is NOT in our string. If it is not in there, then the expression evaluates to true.

```python
if '?' not in str_snake:
    print('no question.')
```

Hey do you NOT have a question mark?

That is True, I indeed don't.

Be careful, characters are case-sensitive! However, we often want to check if letters are the same regardless of case.

We are not the same character!

't' is a distinct character from 'T'.

To get around this, we can use the `s.lower()` function to compare a lowercase version of a string. There is also an `s.upper()` function.

```python
str_snake = '@python!'
uppity_snake = '@PYTHON!'
lower_uppity = uppity_snake.lower()
if lower_uppity == str_snake:
    print("THE SAME CHARACTERS")
```

Our letters are the same and that's what matters!

DON'T FORGET THE PARENTHESES!

Meet the String Snake
Finding some additional characteristics

Note the difference between islower(), which checks if a string/character is all uppercase versus lower() which returns an all lower case version of a string.

```python
is_it_lower = 'T'.islower()
make_it_lower = 'T'.lower()
```

False

'T' islower()

'T' lower() 't'

sees if string is all lower case

returns string that is all lower case

Sometimes, we want to find WHERE a character is in a string. For this, we can use the `s.find()` function.

```python
str_snake.find('!')
```

Where is your exclamation mark?

At index 7!

The function takes in character to look for and returns the INDEX at which it was first found. If nothing was found, it returns -1.

```python
str_snake.find('?')
```

What about your question mark?

-1 ! I don't have one.

There is also the `s.find()` with an optional start and end index parameter.

```python
str_snake.find('n', 0, 3)
```

Is there a 't' in the first 3 characters? If so, where is it?

Negative. Negative one, more precisely.

The end parameter is UBNI the last index!

Often, we need to parse data. In this class, that usually entails looking at a string and extracting a target token. Usually there is a general pattern we follow:

1) Find the beginning character(s) and get start index
2) Get the end index by looping through characters to keep.
3) Return the token w/ start to end index.

Time to parssse!

The first step often entails using the s.find() function on the start character(s) to get the starting index.

```
start = s.find('@')
```

There are often some interesting characters @ the start!

If start isn't found, then we can return something empty as nothing was found.

```
if start == -1:
    return ''
```

Alas, at times there are no such starting characters at all.

For Step 2, we initially set the end index to start plus the length of the start character. This allows us to start searching from where the beginning character(s) finish.

```
end = start + 1
```

Indeed, the end is just the beginning!

Meet the String Snake
Some tips about parssssing

But what if end goes beyond the last index here? This means the token is ONLY made of the beginning character(s). If these characters are to be included in the token, we can return them.

```
if end >= len(s):
    return s[start:]
# returns rest of token
```

Other times, the end is just that: the end!

While we have a character we wish to keep, we increment the end index. This way, end is one beyond the last kept character.

```
# alpha or other character we want
while s[end].isalpha():
    end += 1
```

Keep looping over those we want to keep!

But what if end goes beyond the last index? We would have bad indexing. So we need to FIRST and ALWAYS check that end < len(s).

```
# alpha or other character we want
while end < len(s) and s[end].isalpha():
    end += 1
```

A CLASSIC GUARD! Thank you for protecting me!

ORDER MATTERS WITH the AND OPERATOR.
We must check for a bad index first!

Then comes step 3. Once we have our start and end index, we can retrieve our token by slicing.

```
return s[start:end]
```

TOKEN retrieved

Mr. While LOVES parsing!

Sometimes, start may be start + something if the first characters aren't included.

Additional String Functions

More functions for me, yippee!

Here are some additional string functions which may be helpful in parsing.

my_string.split()

By default, split() divides a string into a list with elements separated by whitespace.

```
s = 'hello my friend'
word_list = s.split()
print(word_list)
# prints ['hello', 'my', 'friend']
```

```
s = '3,1,4,1,5'
num_list = s.split(',')
print(num_list)
# prints ['3','1','4','1','5']
```

Way to chop me up into another type!

You can also add an optional parameter that specifies a delimiter to separate the items. Commas are pretty common.

my_string.strip()

By default, strip() removes the leading and trailing whitespaces of a string.

```
space_s = '    hi   there!  '
s = s.strip(space_s)
print(s)
# prints 'hi   there!'
```

By bye to extra space in the FRONT and BACK!

Often, split is used followed by strip to rid each string of extraneous whitespace.

s.startswith() and s.endswith() check whether a string s begins/ends with a certain substring.

```
s = 'hello!'
s.startswith('h')  # is true
s.endswith('?')  # is false
```

s.replace(old,new) replaces the old substring with the new substring.

```
s = 'mommy'
s = s.replace('o', 'u')
print(s)  # prints mummy
```

```
s = 'mommy'
new_s = s.replace('o', 'u')
print(new_s)  # another way
```

delimeter.join(list) takes in elements of a list and combines them into one string separated by a delimiter (opposite of split function).

```
word_list = ['hello', 'my', 'good', 'friend']
space = ' '
s = space.join(word_list)
print(s)
# prints 'hello my good friend'
```

All of these functions return a NEW string one can STORE in a variable as they can't edit the string in place. This is because the string is what we call "immutable."

```
# THIS DOESN'T WORK
s = 'mommy'
s.replace('o', 'u')
print(s)
# prints mommy
```

Behold Listy the List train! Listy contains a list of values separated by commas. These values can be of any type: characters, strings, integers.

```
empty_list = []
listy = [3, 1, 4]
```

Welcome! Chugg a chugg a choo choo!

Default is to limit items to just one type.

Just like a string, we can get the length and also see if an element is in the list or not.

What's your length?

```
len(listy)
```

I'm three cabooses long!

Is 3 in list?

That is True!

```
if 3 in listy:
```

Is 10 not in list?

That is also True!

```
if 10 not in listy:
```

Listy is also zero-indexed. This means we can index into the list and perform other indexing operations.

```
first_caboose = listy[0]
last_caboose = listy[len(listy) - 1]
```

Here's how to fetch the first and last caboose!

Remember indexing and UBNI!

We can also use slicing operations to create a new list. For example, one might make a new list with the first element removed.

```
all_but_first = listy[1:]
```

Want a list of every element but the first?

I am that new list without the first element!

Meet the Listy the List Train
Taking note of some basic things

We can also loop through Listy with a for i in range loop and for each loop.

```
# both loops print every number in the list
for i in range(len(listy)):
    print(listy[i])  # uses indexing
for num in listy:
    print(num)  # prints elements directly
```

One loops through NUMBERS we use to index, one loops through the elements directly.

If we want to add to the list, we have the append function. We can just do list.append().

```
listy.append(1)
print(listy)
# prints [3, 1, 4, 1]
```

We can do this because lists are mutable. They can be modified in place, unlike strings.

We also have a list.index() function we can use to find the index of an element. Be careful, though—it returns an ERROR if it doesn't find the element.

```
num = listy.index(4)
```

Where is 4 located on the List Train?

It's at index 2!

This is analogous to s.find().

Here are some additional list functions.

```
# retrieves element at last index
last = listy.pop()
# appends new_list's ELEMENTS to listy
listy.extend(new_list)
# creates a NEW list with elements of both lists
list3 = listy + new_list  # listy is not modified
# sorts listy IN PLACE
listy.sort()
```

There's so much you can do with me, Listy! :)

With lists, there are some common patterns to generate new lists and keep track of certain things.

One pattern is to start with a blank list and add on to it based on an original list, known as the accumulate pattern.

For example, we may want to double every element in Listy.

Accumulate Recipe:
1. Declare an empty list to eventually build up
2. Loop through the old list
3. Within it, add conditionally
4. Return the result

```python
def double_list(listy):
    doubles = [] #initialize empty list
    for num in listy:
        # doubles current number
        double = num*2
        # add double to list we're building up
        doubles.append(double)
```

Another pattern is to keep track of the "best" element or value in the list.

For example, we may want to get the max value from the list.

Meet the Listy the List Train
Patterns/Common Recipes

Track recipe
1. Initialize first element as best
2. Loop through list
3. Compare if current element is better than best
4. Return best

```python
def track_highest(listy):
    if len(listy) == 0: # just in case list is empty
        return None
    best = listy[0] # first elem is initial best
    for num in listy: # loop through old list
        if num > best: # update best if current is better
            best = num
    return best
```

Sometimes, you need to keep track of the previous element in a list.

```python
# error if we access empty list
if len(listy) == 0:
    return None
prev = listy[0]
for curr in listy:
    # do something with curr and prev
    prev = curr
```

for each loop

```python
for i in range(1, len(listy)):
    curr = listy[i]
    prev = listy[i - 1]
    # do something with curr and prev
```

for i in range loop

Sometimes, you may see something at the top of the code in all caps like ALPHABET or PI = 3.14159. These are constants we can access in ALL parts of our code.

```python
ALPHABET = ['a', 'b', 'c',
```

Any one of us can access these anytime!

Constants represent stable, unchanging values.

One convention for naming and looping through lists is to name the list something plural and loop through it with a singular variable name.

```python
nums = [3, 1, 4, 1]
for num in nums:
    print(num)
```

If I'm nums, each one of my caboose is a num!

List Comprehensions: Transforming Lists

Sometimes, we just want to update every list element in the same way. For example, we might want to double every element or uppercase every string. Luckily, we can do that with list comprehensions! These dense lines of code can give us a new list with each of the old elements transformed.

```python
def double_list(nums):
    doubles = [num*2 for num in nums]
    return doubles
```

num*2
On the left, we describe what to do with each list item. In this case, the list item name, defined by the right side, is num, and we are doubling each num.

for num in nums
On the right, we NAME a variable to represent each list item. Here, each item is named num. We can change this name as long as it's consistent.

doubles

```python
# turns each word in list to all uppercase
def upper_case(words):
    uppers = [word.upper() for word in words]
    return uppers
```

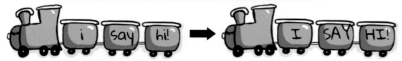

```python
# squares each number in a list
def square_list(nums):
    squares = [num*num for num in nums]
    return squares
```

We can also add an if statement to conditionally include elements in the new list. It ELIMINATES elements that don't satisfy the condition.

```python
def three_is_max(nums):
    three_max = [num for num in nums if num <= 3]
    return three_max
```

So four didn't make the cut. Sad to see her go.

Remember how Program is secretly made up of functions? There is actually one function at the bottom of the code that calls everything else! Behold, Queen Main!

```
def main():
    # (provided)
    args = sys.argv[1:]
```

If you've ever seen this code before, 'tis the work of moi!

When you run a program in the terminal, Queen Main also runs. But what does she take in?

`python3 ghost.py`

When you run this, you implicitly call me, one of the most important functions of all!

She usually takes in arguments DIRECTLY from the terminal. It's one of her royal powers and why she's dubbed Queen of Args!

```
def main():
    # (provided)
    args = sys.argv[1:]
```

My special powers!!!

When you type in inputs after the python3 in the terminal, each input is stored as a string in a LIST. Queen Main often uses this list, accessed with sys.argv.

`python3 ghost.py clock-tower`

sys.argsv is ['ghost.py', 'clock-tower']

Even the terminal inputs can transform into a Listy Train!

MAIN
Queen of Args

You may see args = argsv[1:]. This is list slicing! It excludes the first element of argsv (the file name, e.g. 'ghost.py').

```
% python3 ghost.py clock-tower
def main():
    # (provided)|
    args = sys.argv[1:]
    print(args)
    print(sys.argv)

['clock-tower']
['ghost.py', 'clock-tower']
```

Get me the user arguments that actually change!

In this class, we usually already know the program file name and want variable info.

We can then use these arguments in our user functions as necessary, indexing as with a normal list.

```
def main():
    # (provided)
    args = sys.argv[1:]
    filename = args[0]
    doSomething(filename)
```

Remember the first element is at index 0!

We often have to do some error checking to make sure the user inputs are valid.

```
def main():
    # (provided)
    args = sys.argv[1:]
    # error checking if we are expecting
    # only one user argument
    if len(args) > 1:
        return
    filename = args[0]
    doSomething(filename)
```

I can still malfunction, you know!

In CS106A, this is often done by length checking and matching words/placement.

That's Main, Queen of Args!

I am powerful, aren't I, darling :)?

Often, if we are running a program with many functions that rely on each other, we'll want to make sure that each of these functions work. But how to do so?

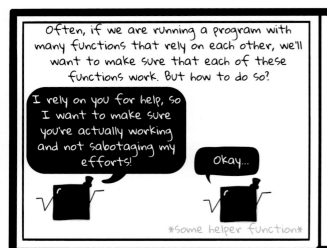

I rely on you for help, so I want to make sure you're actually working and not sabotaging my efforts!

Okay...

Some helper function

Meet Doc Test! They like to experiment with the code and make sure things are a-okay. We can test our functions with Doc Test, who is awesome for debugging!

Doc Test is found in the function comment, a multiline comment in all green surrounded by triple quotes.

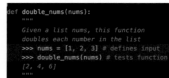

```
def double_nums(nums):
    """
    Given a list nums, this function
    doubles each number in the list
    >>> nums = [1, 2, 3] # defines input
    >>> double_nums(nums) # tests function
    [2, 4, 6]
    """
```

I am surrounded by lines of green!

Doc Test itself is defined by >>>. We can define our inputs, write the function to test, and then write the expected output.

```
def double_nums(nums):
    """
    Given a list nums, this function
    doubles each number in the list
    >>> nums = [1, 2, 3] # defines input
    >>> double_nums(nums) # tests function
    [2, 4, 6]
    """
```

I merely indicate whether your function produces the output you expect.

Doc Test
Testing the limits of our functions

One way to run Doc Test is to right-click, then click them off the menu. If Doc Test gives us the green check mark, our tests passed!

Click me, run me if you wanna reach me, when ya wanna test code, it's ok.

If Doc Test gives us a yellow x, that means there is a difference between our code output and the expected output. We can then examine this difference.

```
Test Results                  Tests failed: 1, passed: 1 of 2 tests
  Test Results                 0ms
    double_nums                0ms   Failure
                                     <Click to see difference>

Failed example:
    double_nums(nums) # tests function
Expected:
    [2, 4, 6]
Got:
    [[1, 2, 3, 1, 2, 3], [1, 2, 3, 1, 2, 3]]
```

My results indicate that you may have made a mistake in your function!

SOME THINGS TO WATCH FOR!

- beware of spaces, especially in lists
- double-check that you have the correct EXPECTED OUTPUT
- sometimes the function is correct but not Doc Test

I merely take in your input and output to experiment with!

Just because Doc Test is all green doesn't mean our function is good to go. Testing doesn't guarantee our function works; it only makes us surer.

Test the limits! Craft inputs that stretch the code in hopes of strengthening it!

Because of this THOROUGH edge case testing is VERY important.

Sometimes, we'll have an external file that we'll want to use in our code. Files, however, are usually stored as their filenames, which are mere strings.

'super-secret-stuff.txt'

So, we somehow need to open the file so that we can go through its contents. We can do so with the following command:

```
open(filename)
```

I'm opened and ready to be read!

before

after

We can go through the file line by line, storing its contents in a variable like f and then going through each line of the file.

```
with open(filename) as f:
    for line in f:
        print(line)
```

closed   open   closed

The with keyword opens the file for as long as necessary and then closes it so that we don't have to! Convenient!

We can use readlines() to read the file into a list. Here, each line of the file is an item of a list.

```
lines = f.readlines()
# prints first line in file
print(lines[0])
```

Welcome aboard to the train from file!

File reading and input
Some miscellaneous things

After reading a line, we'll often split up the words into a list and then proceed from there, or apply a function to each line.

```
with open(filename) as f:
    for line in f:
        words = line.split()
```

```
with open(filename) as f:
    for line in f:
        print(line)
```

Each line can be treated as a string!

Let's now look at how we might get an input from the user with the input() function. This function takes in a user prompt and returns the answer to that prompt.

prompt to give user   user's response in a string

input()

It's perfect for interacting with users and making responsive code!

```
390    def double_my_num():
391        num = input("Hello! Type in a whole number! ")
```

```
Terminal:  Local  ×  +
Hello! Type in a whole number! 3
```

The terminal can talk to both the code and user!

Here's an example: Often times we'll need to convert the input if we want to use it as another type like an int.

```
def double_my_num():
    num = input("Hello! Type in a whole number! ")
    num = int(num)
    print("Your number doubled is ", num*2)
```

```
Terminal:  Local  ×  +
Hello! Type in a whole number! 3
Your number doubled is  6
```

Pretty cool, eh?

Chapter Five
DRAWING WITH CODE
But a Canvas to Our Imaginations

Mr. Canvas

O. Val

Rectangela

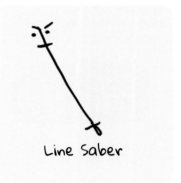

Line Saber

Fill O. Val

Fill Rectangela

Draw String

At the intersection of art and code lies Mr. Canvas! He loves art so much that he has become the canvas.

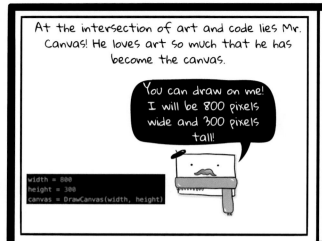

You can draw on me! I will be 800 pixels wide and 300 pixels tall!

```
width = 800
height = 300
canvas = DrawCanvas(width, height)
```

Just like with grids and pixels, Mr. Canvas grows down, his canvas starting at 0,0 in the upper left. Since Mr. Canvas is zero-indexed, his corners are one less than the dimension length.

(0,0)   (799,0)

(0,299)   (799,299)

Mr. Canvas has PREDEFINED friends called in the canvas.function() format just like bit and pixel. OTHER functions have to take in Mr. Canvas as an input parameter.

```
canvas.draw
# c    draw_rect(self, x, y, width, height, color)
       draw_line(self, x1, y1, x2, y2, color)
# Y    draw_oval(self, x, y, width, height, color)
       draw_string(self, x, y, text, color)

       canvas.fill
       # can   fill_oval(self, x, y, width...
              fill_rect(self, x, y, width...
```

This is because I am imported!

In general, functions with Mr. Canvas take in a left and top coordinate from the canvas in addition to a width and height.

Sometimes, my canvas is shifted from 0,0!

Meet Mr. Canvas
An artistic icon

But why aren't the top and left always at (0,0)? Instead of using up the entire canvas, we often break it up into mini-canvases with the same image or repeating patterns.

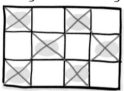

```
# canvas is 800x300 pixels
# sub width is 800//4 = 200 pixels
# sub height is 300//3 = 100 pixels
```

Each of these mini-canvases has a different starting point on the actual canvas.

I start at (0,0)

My left is at 200, top at (200,100)

I start at (400, 200).

Mr. Canvas's drawing functions need to know the coordinates at which to begin their drawing shenanigans and how tall and wide they should be.

If you're going to draw ovals on us, you should know where exactly to start!

The subwidth and subheight give us more information on the dimensions of these mini canvases, also useful for the drawing functions.

If you're going to draw ovals on us, you should know how wide and high we each are!

Indeed, Mr. Canvas comes with many in-built drawing functions. As he doesn't do the drawings himself, he has many friends to help fulfill him.

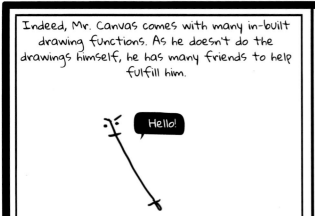

Hello!

One of these friends is the line saber, aka draw_line.

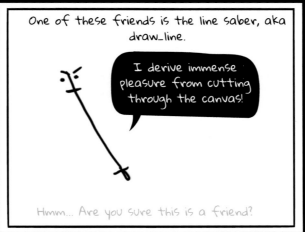

I derive immense pleasure from cutting through the canvas!

Hmm... Are you sure this is a friend?

Generally speaking, line saber takes in two coordinates represented by x1, y1 (sometimes left and top) and x2, y2. The line saber then draws a line between the two points.

`canvas.draw_line(x1, y1, x2, y2)`

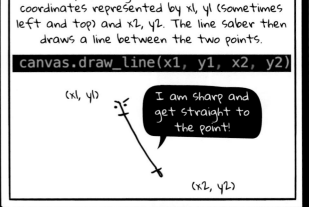

(x1, y1)

I am sharp and get straight to the point!

(x2, y2)

Another friend is Rectangela, or draw_rect. She draws a rectangle of width and height starting at a coordinate x,y.

`canvas.draw_rect(x1, y1, width, height)`

I will paint a nice rectangle outline. I'm often used to outline mini canvases!

Meet Mr. Canvas
A friendship overview

Another friend is the closely related O. Val, or draw_oval. She draws an oval of width and height bounded by a rectangle starting at coordinate x, y of width and height.

`canvas.draw_oval(x1, y1, width, height)`

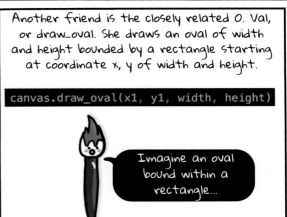

Imagine an oval bound within a rectangle...

Rectangela, O. Val, and Line Saber take in an optional color= parameter to determine the shade of the OUTLINE.

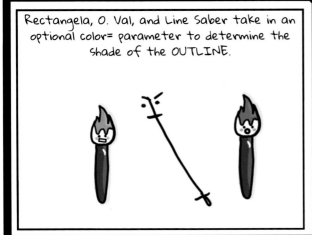

Since Rectangela and O. Val both do just an outline, there is also fill_oval and fill_rect that draw and fill in their respective shapes with a color.

We are very filling!

To call these function friends, we have to calculate where the x and y coordinates should be relative to the canvas. This often involves some math.

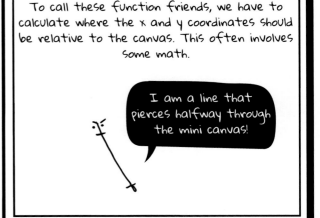

I am a line that pierces halfway through the mini canvas!

1

Let's look at Line Saber. One common pattern for them is to draw a series of evenly-spaced lines up and down the canvas. This requires a bit of math for the spacing!

We too will be in the context of the mini-canvas!

Let's take this spiderweb pattern. It's n = 4 lines, all going from the upper left corner to evenly spaced spots on the right side of the canvas.

The number of lines is usually represented by n!

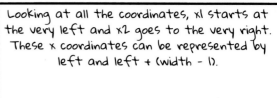

width = 200
height = 100

Looking at all the coordinates, x1 starts at the very left and x2 goes to the very right. These x coordinates can be represented by left and left + (width - 1).

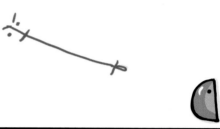

Here, the y-coordinates involve more math. Although the first y-coordinate begins at the top, we have to figure out how to evenly space the second y-coordinate out.

SECOND Y-COORDINATE

Starts at top. Line 1/4

Middle are lines 2/4 and lines 3/4

Ends at bottom. Line 4/4

Mr. Canvas's friends
Looking at Line Saber

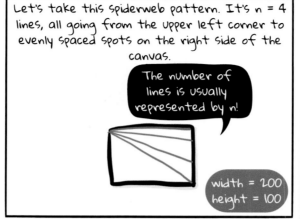

Notice that even though there are FOUR (n) lines, the space is divided into THREE (n - 1). This means we can add something to y three times to hit each coordinate (y_add).

SECOND Y-COORDINATE

Line 1 is 0/3 of the height. (0)

Lines 2 and 3 are at 1/3 and 2/3 of the height. (33 and 66)

Line 4 is at 3/3 of the height. (99)

Once we have the fraction of the canvas (0/3, 1/3, 2/3, 3/3) we need to multiply it by the max height to get the exact COORDINATE.

```
for i in range(n): # n is total num of lines
    frac_of_canvas = i/(n-1)
    max_y_coord = height - 1
    y_add = frac_of_canvas*max_y_coord
    canvas.draw_line(left, top, left + width - 1, y_add)
```

REMEMBER TO ADD LEFT AND TOP.

For both x and y, this is an important pattern to know!

```
for i in range(n):
    frac = i/(n - 1)
    max_y = height - 1
    y_add = frac*max_y
```

```
for i in range(n):
    frac = i/(n - 1)
    max_x = width - 1
    x_add = frac*max_x
```

This is coding cannon!

There are also additional functions like draw_string()!

hello :)

More on Mr.Canvas and friends can be found here!

6

PYTHON PERSONALITY TEST
WHAT'S YOUR OBJECT TYPE?

Bit

you like to move-it move-it and turn the beat around even though you may be a little bit uncoordinated and require the assistance of others

Grid

you are super-duper accommodating but know where to set your boundaries; you are assertive but also very accepting

Pixel

you love to socialize and constantly change things up and can suss out people's true colors before you even meet them

Canvas

you're super-duper artistic, individualistic, and have a beginner's mind when it comes to learning, allowing you to picture anything

Chapter Six
MORE ON ITERABLES
Dictionaries, Tuples, Lambda, and Some Helpful Functions

Explorer Dict

Sir Tuple

Madam Lambda

Meet Explorer Dict the dictionary, a new data type, declared with curly brackets!

```
my_dict = {}
```

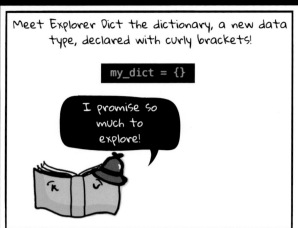

I promise so much to explore!

Python dictionaries are made up of a series of key-value pairs, similar to how regular dictionaries are made up of pairs of words and definitions. Each key maps to one value.

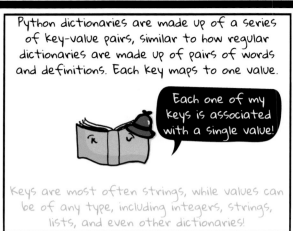

Each one of my keys is associated with a single value!

Keys are most often strings, while values can be of any type, including integers, strings, lists, and even other dictionaries!

Here's an example of a dictionary mapping some countries to capital cities.

```
capital_cities = {"USA": "Washington. D.C.",
                  "Mexico": "Mexico City",
                  "Sierra Leone": "Freetown",
                  "Honduras": "Tegucigalpa",
                  "India": "New Delhi",
                  "Burkina Faso": "Ouagadougou"
                  }
```

What can I say? I possess worldly knowledge.

To access a value, we must use its key in the following format.

```
capital_cities["Sierra Leone"]  # gets Freetown

# generally this pattern is dict[key]
```

My values are locked unless you have the right keys!

Explorer Dict doesn't have any numbered indexes.

~ Meet Explorer Dict ~
Discovering the world of keys and values

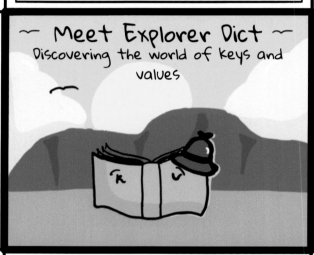

With this notation, we can now access the values. But be careful: if a key doesn't exist and we try to store its value, you'll have an error on your hands!

```
city1 = capital_cities["Sierra Leone"]
city2 = capital_cities["Scotland"]
```

```
    city2 = capital_cities["Scotland"]
KeyError: 'Scotland'
```

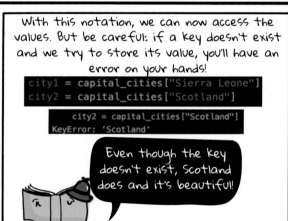

Even though the key doesn't exist, Scotland does and it's beautiful!

To avoid this, before accessing a value, we'll want to check whether its key exists in the dictionary first. This is similar to the syntax for lists and strings.

```
if "Scotland" in capital_cities:
    capital = capital_cities["Scotland"]
    print(capital)
```

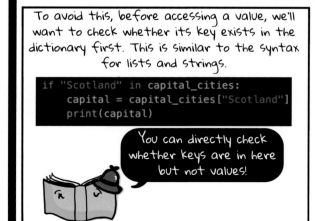

You can directly check whether keys are in here but not values!

If the key is not in the dictionary and we still want to do the same task, we can add it and then proceed as normal.

```
if "Scotland" in capital_cities:
    print(capital_cities)
else:
    capital_cities["Scotland"] = "Edinburgh"
    print(capital_cities)
```

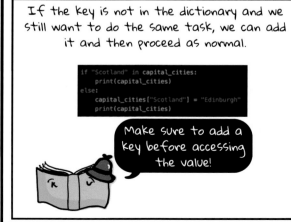

Make sure to add a key before accessing the value!

A more efficient way to refactor the code, however, would be to add Scotland first, and then do the task just once.

```
if "Scotland" not in capital_cities:
    capital_cities["Scotland"] = "Edinburgh"
print(capital_cities["Scotland"])
```

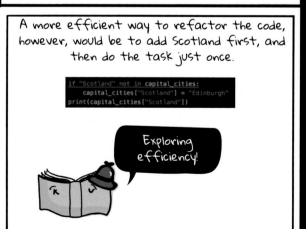

Exploring efficiency!

One common type of dictionary we might have is a counts dictionary. The goal here is to keep count of how many times we have something.

```
counts = {}
```

I'm keeping count of something. I just don't know what yet.

For example, we might want to keep count of how many times each letter pops up in a word.

```
def calculate_counts(word):
    counts = {}
```

Hello, I'm counts!

We usually name a Dict after its values.

One approach to do this is to:
1) Loop through each character in the word
2) If the character is not in the dictionary add it with a count of 1
3) If it is in the dictionary, increment the existing value by 1

```
def calculate_counts(word):
    counts = {}
    for ch in word:  # step 1
        if ch in counts:  # step 2
            counts[ch] += 1
        else:  # step 3
            counts[ch] = 1
```

Once again, we can refactor the code. We can check if the key is not in the dictionary and if so, add a default value. We can then proceed as normal.

```
for ch in word:
    if ch not in counts:
        counts[ch] = 0
    counts[ch] += 1
```

The default value is one that serves as a placeholder type we can add to later. For strings and lists this value is often "" or [].

~ Meet Explorer Dict ~
Finding out which value maps to which key in the wild

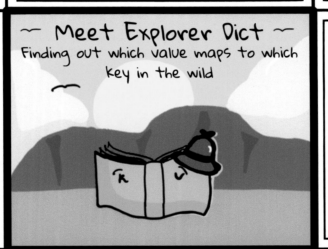

NOTE that if we store the integer in a variable and then increment that, we won't actually be incrementing the number. This is because we'll be working with only a copy!

```
for ch in word:
    if ch not in counts:
        counts[ch] = 0
    curr_count = counts[ch]
    curr_count += 1
```

Although curr_count does increase, the number in the counts dictionary does not.

This problem applies to types like integers and strings, but this is actually a different story for lists and dictionaries.

```
# appends counts to list
for ch in word:
    if ch not in counts:
        counts[ch] = []
    curr_count = counts[ch]
    curr_count.append(1)
```

We're SPECIAL.

Hmmph...

Because of how Python stores these large types, if we make any changes to a list/dict they persist, even as an external variable

Copies are really expensive nowadays!

Haven't they always been?

This is because if we set something equal to the list, it points to the same list in memory. So it's never creating a copy but always dealing with the list itself!

counts['a']

list = counts['a']

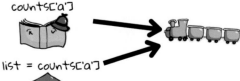

More on this can be found on page 4 of ch 1.

How might we further edit dictionaries where the values are lists or other dictionaries (nested dicts)? There's the key, but the value is also this complex type with which we can do so much more.

I complicate things!

What if we wanted to make a map of letters to words in a list that started with each letter?

```
def build_first_letters(words):
    """
    input: [ward, mine, moon, word, book]
    result: {'w': ["ward", "word"],
             'm': ["mine", "moon"],
             'b': ["book"]
    """
```

Let's assume every word in the list is unique.

We could follow the same structure as before, checking if the key is not in the dictionary. If that's the case, then we add a default value...

```
def build_first_letters(words):
    first_letters = {}
    for word in words:
        first_letter = word[0]
        if first_letter not in first_letters:
            first_letters[first_letter] = []
```

This is followed by UPDATING the value, which is a list. We can then grab the list and append to it. And then eventually RETURN the dictionary.

```
def build_first_letters(words):
    first_letters = {}
    for word in words:
        first_letter = word[0]
        if first_letter not in first_letters:
            first_letters[first_letter] = []
        word_list = first_letters[first_letter]
        word_list.append(word)
```

We can technically do first_letters[first_letter].append(word) but the initial way is better for readability!

~ Meet Explorer Dict ~
The key to nested data structures

What if we mapped each letter to ANOTHER dictionary? This INNER dictionary maps a word to a count of the times it pops up in the list.

```
def build_first_letters2(words):
    """
    input: [ward, mine, moon, word, ward, book]
    result: {'w': {"ward": 2, "word": 1},
             'm': ["mine": 1, "moon": 1],
             'b': ["book": 1]
    """
```

Let's drop the assumption that every word in the list is unique.

The beautiful thing is once we get the inner dictionary, we can treat it like any other dictionary, following our usual patterns.

```
first_letters = {}
for word in words:
    first_letter = word[0]
    if first_letter not in first_letters:
        first_letters[first_letter] = {}
    inner_counts_dict = first_letters[first_letter]
```

Alas, the familiarity of retrieving the value and the novelty of it being another dictionary...

And then follow the general pattern.

```
first_letters = {}
for word in words:
    first_letter = word[0]
    if first_letter not in first_letters:
        first_letters[first_letter] = {}
    inner_counts_dict = first_letters[first_letter]

    if word not in inner_counts_dict:
        inner_counts_dict[word] = 0
    inner_counts_dict += 1
```

Followed by the familiarity of dealing with a dictionary!

There are also some additional functions with dictionaries to get a list-like* such as d.keys(), d.items() and d.values().

my_dict.values() allows you to finally loop through my values directly!

*Technically, these functions return a list-like. You can use the list() function to get a list.

Meet a new type called Sir Tuple, declared with parentheses. We must specify Sir Tuple's elements when we declare 'im because of his fixed size. He is eccentric in that he often stores elements of different types!

```
tup = (1, 'a')
```

Sir Tuple is like a list in the sense that you can index into the different elements. and store them...

```
firstLetter = tup[1]
```

We are SOMEWHAT alike...

But there are a few important differences, most notably the fixed size and elements.

Nah nah nah nah nah, you can't change me!

Side Note: Just like Python strings, tuples are immutable.

This means we can't change the size or edit the tuple directly.

```
# very much NOT allowed
tup[0] = 0
```

Oh! We're kind of different then...

Meet Sir Tuple
An eccentric, immutable type of many different elements

Because of this fixed quality, tuples like Sir Tuple can be useful for things like ordered pairs and storing data like ratings.

```
coordTup = (x, y, z)
originTup = (0, 0)
```

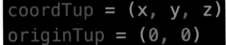

If we want to change a value within a tuple, we have to rebuild it. Occasionally, this involves creating a list and converting it into a tuple.

```
coordList = [0, 1, 1]
newCoordTup = tuple(coordList)
```

Here are some differences between when to use tuples and lists.

Tuple	List
• a few elems	• unlimited elems
• fixed number of elems	• can append more elements
• may have diff types	• generally the same type
• can be dict key	• cannot be dict key

As we'll see, tuples are a list-like. By default, if you sort them they are sorted by their first element with later elements used as tiebreakers.

With me, you'll see all sorts of new things!

Wouldn't it be nice to automatically apply a function to EVERY element of a list-like?

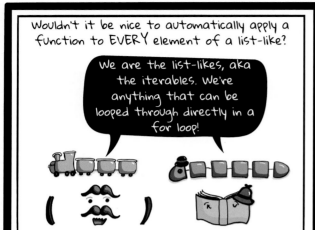

We are the list-likes, aka the iterables. We're anything that can be looped through directly in a for loop!

For this, we have Mr. Map Function. He takes in a function and a list-like. The function gets applied to EACH ELEMENT of the list-like.

```
def double_num(num):
    return num*2
def double_123list():
    my_list = [1, 2, 3]
    map(double_num, my_list)
```

function, list-like

new list-like with fn applied to all elems

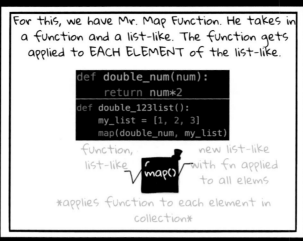

map()

applies function to each element in collection

Map returns a strange input, so in order to get that input back in list form, we transform it into a list with the list() function.

```
list(map(double_num, my_list))
```

weird map object

Ahh, back to my good ol' self!

list()

Transforms input to list

Next, meet Madam Lambda and her Lambdas. They are single lines of code that embody the tasks of functions.

```
double_n = lambda n: n*2
double_n(4)   # evaluates to 8
```

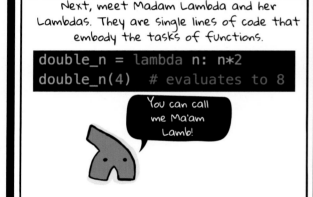

You can call me Ma'am Lamb!

Madam Lambda
A strong, powerful type

The lambda keyword indicates that we're about to define a lambda. The left side defines our input and the right side defines what to do with that input.

```
lambda n: n*2
```
```
def double_n(n):
    return n*2
```

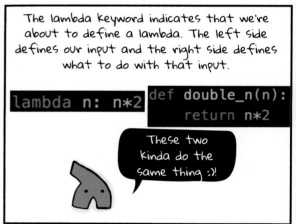

These two kinda do the same thing :)!

With the map function, instead of passing in a predefined function, we can actually just pass in Ma'am Lamb right then and there!

```
list(map(lambda n: n*2, my_list))
```

Remember that this lambda will be applied to EACH element of the list-like.

Generally speaking, since Ma'am Lamb is limited to working out on one line, she's good for transforming certain inputs.

My strength is in agility—quick transformations!

Regular functions are still great for having helper functions, multiple lines, if statements, variables, loops, comments, and loops, however. But one-liners are really cool!

We all work in harmony!

FUNctions with collections:
sorted, min, and max

   ( )

Now that we've encountered many list-like collections, what functions might be available?

sorted()

This function sorts a collection in INCREASING order, returning a new sorted version of the collection.

```
# usage: sorted(list_like)
string_list = ['b', 'a', 'c']
int_list = [3, 1, 4, 1, 5, 9]
# prints ['a', 'b', 'c']
print(sorted(string_list))
# prints [1, 1, 3, 4, 5, 9]
print(sorted(int_list))
```

There is an optional parameter called reverse that allows us to REVERSE sort elements, that is, sort them in DECREASING order.

```
# usage: sorted(list_like, reverse=True)
string_list = ['b', 'a', 'c']
int_list = [3, 1, 4, 1, 5, 9]
# prints ['c', 'b', 'a']
print(sorted(string_list, reverse=True))
# prints [9, 5, 4, 3, 1, 1]
print(sorted(int_list, reverse=True))
```

By default, integers are ordered by size and strings are ordered alphabetically with one special twist: UPPERCASE letters come FIRST.

THE KEY PARAMETER
For all three of these functions, we can OVERRIDE the default sorting criteria with the KEY parameter. Just like reverse=True, we can say key= and insert our criteria that defines how to sort things. One way we can define this criteria is with a lambda function. This lambda will be used to compare each element.

KEY PARAMETER EXAMPLE:

```
strings = ['four', 'z', 'to']
# prints out list by string length
# new list will be ['z', 'to', 'for']
print(sorted(strings, key=lambda x: len(x)))
```

min()

This function returns the lowest value from a list-like.

```
# usage: min(list_like)
string_list = ['b', 'a', 'c']
int_list = [3, 1, 4, 1, 5, 9]
# prints 'a'
print(min(string_list))
# prints 1
print(min(int_list))
```

max()

This function returns the highest value from a list-like.

```
# usage: max(list_like)
string_list = ['b', 'a', 'c']
int_list = [3, 1, 4, 1, 5, 9]
# prints 'c'
print(max(string_list))
# prints 9
print(max(int_list))
```

 We can use all of these functions with d.keys(), d.items(), and d.values(), which actually return list-likes!

CS106A

You got through the CS106A side of the comic! It was quite the journey :)! Every Bit proud of ya!

CONGRATS

START

First, we journeyed through the basics and fundamentals like functions, variables, and integers.

We learned how to get a little more control over the state of our program...

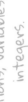 

Then we jumped into some serious Python with strings and lists and such...

...followed by a splash of color and range of artistic expressions.

...followed by even more artistic expression with Mr. Canvas and his friends.

Finally, we learned about some powerful new types.

 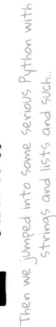     

FINISH

Hopefully, the coding journey will continue!

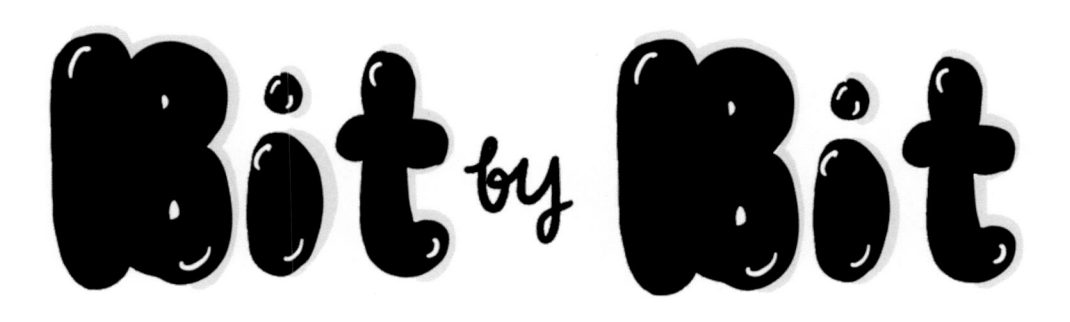

Bit by Bit

A GRAPHIC INTRODUCTION TO COMPUTER SCIENCE

Ecy Femi King

Stanford University Press
Stanford, California

CS106B

Fractal Grid of Contents

CS106B

Fractal Grid of Contents

Chapter One
- Python to C++
- Variables in C++
- Functions in C++
- Strings in C++
- Qt Creator
- Control Flow in C++
- Debugging and Style
- Reference

Chapter Two
- Vectors
- Grids
- Queues
- Stacks
- Sets
- Maps

Chapter Three
- Big-O
- Efficiency
- Recursion
- Backtracking

Chapter Four
- Memory
- Pointers
- The Call Stack
- The Heap
- New
- Delete
- Structs

Chapter Five
- Classes
- User vs Client
- Header Files
- .cpp files

Chapter Six
- Linked Lists
- Trees

???
- C++ Personality Test
- Certificate of Bilingualism
- Fragman
- Sunglasses

Chapter One
I CAN C++ NOW
Examining C++isms and Basics

Sir Python Snake

C++ Camel, Esquire

Variable

Function

The String Snake

The Control Flow Family

Doc and Reference

Lady de Bug

Going from Python to C++ can be intimidating! For one, even simple operators look VERY different.

"or and not"

"|| && !"

There are also many style and syntax differences.

snake_case!

camelCase!

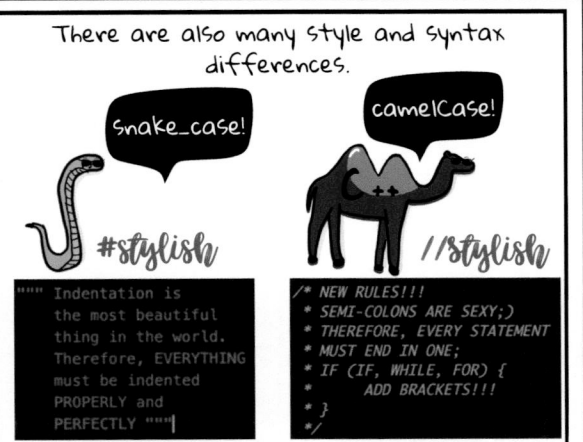

#stylish

//stylish

""" Indentation is the most beautiful thing in the world. Therefore, EVERYTHING must be indented PROPERLY and PERFECTLY """|

```
/* NEW RULES!!!
* SEMI-COLONS ARE SEXY;)
* THEREFORE, EVERY STATEMENT
* MUST END IN ONE;
* IF (IF, WHILE, FOR) {
*      ADD BRACKETS!!!
* }
*/
```

Remember Function and Variable from CS106A?

Remember us? Of course you do! Alas, we have changed!

If you're seeing us for the first time, I'm Variable and on the left is Function!

In C++, all functions and variables have the return type spelled out at the time of declaration.

int sum()

```
int sum(int x, int y) {
    int theSum = x + y;
    return theSum;
}
```

The def keyword is replaced with Function's return type, and Variable now has its own type written out when defined.

Transitioning from Python to C++
It may be a long and arduous journey!

Imports— the predefined packages that come with all sorts of programming essentials and goodies— look a little different too. They allow us to use certain functions and even types such as strings.

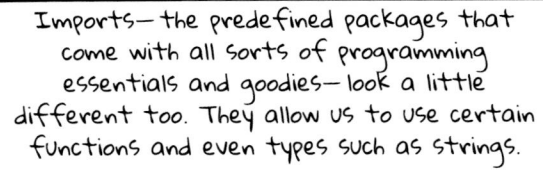

```
#include "console.h"
#include "strlib.h"
#include "map.h"
```

Imports like to bring along friends...

#include <string>

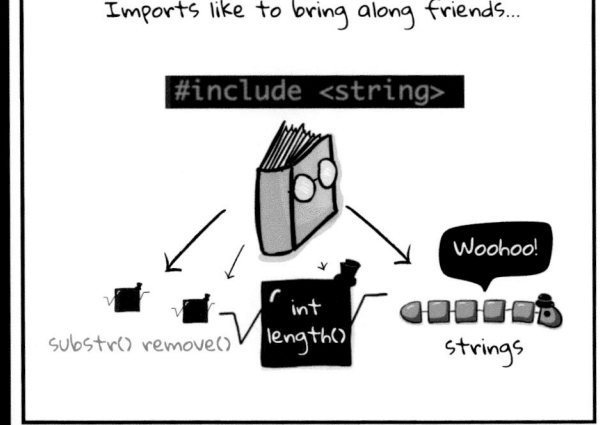

substr() remove()   int length()   Woohoo!

strings

Although there are many differences, many things remain the same. One example is reassigning a variable.

```
int tripleSum = theSum;
tripleSum = theSum*3;
```

Still, other things take some getting used to, but don't worry. You'll get the hang of it, soon enough!

General differences

high-level, abstract
easier to learn
slower
interpreted (translated line by line)

// low-level language
// learning curve
// faster
// compiled (translated into machine code all at once)

STYLE AND SYNTAX

Python	C++
# a comment	
""" multiple lines """	
and, or, not, ==	
True/False	

FUNCTIONS AND VARIABLES

Python	C++

# snake case 	
my_function()
my_var = 2	

# var_name = val 	
x = -2
x += 1
x += 5	

def my_function(x):
    x += 1
    return x	

CONTROL STATEMENTS

Python	C++
if x > 0: x += 1	
for i in range(2): print(i)	
for ch in str: print(ch)	
while x < 0: x += 1	

STRINGS

Python	C++
s = "hi" + " all"	
s = "hi all"	
s[1] = "p"	
ch = s[1]	
len(s)	
s[len(s) - 1]	

Python to C++ Scavenger Hunt

Find the equivalent C++ code from Python!

STRINGS, PART 2

s[3:] # "all"	
s[:3] # "hi "	
s = "abcdefg" s[1:4] # "bcd"	
s[a:b]	
s[a:]	
s[:b]	
s[-1]	

STRINGS, PART 3

Python	C++
index = s.find(substr) if index != -1: print("Found at", index)	
if substr in s: print("Substr is:", substr)	

Do you prefer me or that snake of a language? As time goes on, you may be surprised by how things change...

Head to the end of the chapter for solutions!

Hints!

DATA TYPES

list []	
dictionary {}	

Remember the string snake? It is still made up of a bunch of characters STRUNG together. But now, there are some noticeable differences.

```
string cppSnake = "snakes";
```

First, to get to the string snake's length, we now have a different function, length()!

The len() function is soooooo Python 3.7

```
//evaluates to 6
cppSnake.length();
```

In C++ we'll see lots of functions of the form noun.verb() or object.function().

To access a character, we can still index into it, aka do myString[i].

```
char myFavChar = cppSnake[4];
```

NOTE: In C++, strings are now represented by double quotes, and characters are now represented by single quotes.

I would host you but... you're no longer my type.

```
char aSingleB = 'b';
char angryB = "b";        o Cann
string buzzingB = 'b';    o
string  doubleQuoteB= "b";
```

Revisiting Strings in C++
The String Snake travels to C++ city

Compared to Python, we also have a new ability! We can change the string snake's values directly! Since string[i] is a character, we MUST also use single quotes.

Each one of us is a character!!!

```
cppSnake[1] = "t";     o
cppSnake[1] = 't';
```

Recall that in Python, strings were immutable. This meant we couldn't edit the string snake; we could only replace it.

Python snake: Please don't change me! Create a new string if you will.

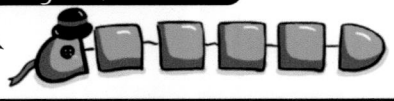

```
stringSnake[1] = "t"
TypeError: 'str' object does not support item assignment
```

But in C++, things are different now!

```
cppSnake[0] ='p';
```
Mix and match me as you please!

```
cppSnake[1] ='l';
```

```
cppSnake[3] ='t';
```
I must admit, I'm a bit hungry now!

C++ CHEAT CODE: You can use string.back() to get the last character in a string instead of the string[str.length() - 1].

```
cppSnake[cppSnake.length() - 1] = 'd';
cppSnake.back() = 'd'; //same thing
```

```
char lastChar = cppSnake[cppSnake.length() - 1];
char easyLastChar = cppSnake.back();
```

So have you got my back now?

To loop through each character of the string snake, we can do a range loop...

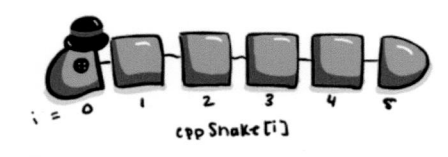

```
for (int i = 0; i < cppSnake.length(); i++)
char currentChar = cppSnake[i];
cout << currentChar;
}
```

...or do a for each loop

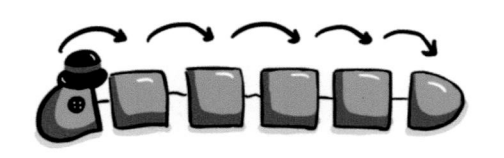

```
for (char currentChar: cppSnake) {
    cout << currentChar;
}
```

In C++, we also have a new limitation. We can't add two string literals with a plus sign, that is "bare strings" + "like this".

no string snake, no service

```
string cppSnake2 = "cpp" + "snake";
```

We can, however, add a literal to an existing string.

```
string cppString = "cpp";
string cppSnake2 = cppString + "Snake";
```

Revisiting Strings in C++
Noting some unique characteristics

...and also use += notation.

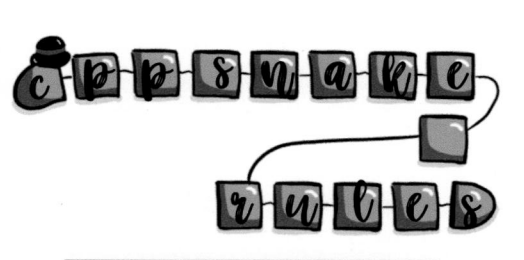

```
cppString += " rules";
```

same as cppString = cppString + " rules"

We can also add a character to a string because C++ says so.

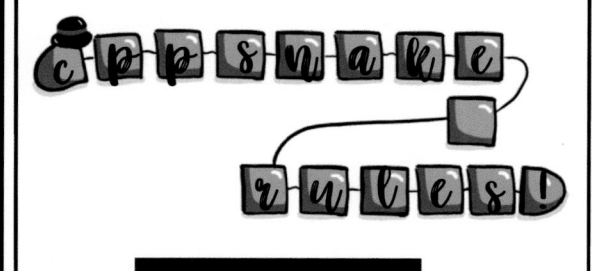

```
cppString += '!';
```

We can also use the function empty() to see if our string is empty.

Feeling empty indeed...

```
bool isStringEmpty = cppString.empty()
```

Several more cool functions are available here.

Because we can edit the string snake directly instead of building another one up, there are a lot of cool new functions at our disposal.

```
erase()    substr()
```

Let's first look at the erase function. Its first argument is the position to start erasing from. All characters from that index are erased.

Imma So Smol now!

```
cppSnake.erase(1);
```

The second, optional argument is the LENGTH to erase from the starting index.

```
cppSnake = "snakes";
// erases 2 characters, starting from index 2
cppSnake.erase(2,2);
```
This second, optional parameter is NOT an index!

Be careful: Once you use the erase function, the ORIGINAL string is MODIFIED, even if you don't store the value in a variable! This can do A LOT of damage if you don't know.

```
string oldStr = "past string";
string newStr = oldStr.erase(1,7);
```

newStr   oldStr

```
cout << newStr << endl; //prints "ping"
cout << oldStr << endl; //prints "ping" TOO
```

Revisiting Strings in C++
Substring and Erase Functions

Noting Some Unique characteristics

Let's now look at the substr() function. Its first argument is also the position to start the substring from.

Off with my head huh!

```
cppSnake = "snakes";
cppSnake = cppSnake.substr(1);
```

The second argument is the LENGTH to make the substring. Compare this to the erase function with the same arguments.

```
cppSnake = "snakes";
cppSnake.substr(2,2);
```

THIS SECOND PARAMETER IS DIFFERENT FROM THE INDEX!!!

UNLIKE PYTHON, the second parameter IS NOT THE INDEX. Let's compare the C++ substring function to splicing in Python.

- s.substr(1, 2)
- s.substr(a, b - a)
- s.substr(3)
- s.substr(a)
- s.substr(0, 3)
- s.substr(0, b)

- s[1:3]
- s[a:b]
- s[3:]
- s[a:]
- s[:3]
- s[:b]

Unlike erase, substring leaves the original string unchanged.

```
string oldStr = "past string";
string newStr = oldStr.substr(1,7);
```

newStr   oldStr

Just a little reminder for s.erase and s.substring...

The second, optional argument is the LENGTH to erase from the starting index. This is DIFFERENT from the INDEX to END at. Again, for the second parameter...

THIS IS NOT THE INDEX

THIS IS NOT THE INDEX

THIS IS NOT THE INDEX

THIS IS NOT THE INDEX

THIS IS NOT THE INDEX

THIS IS NOT THE INDEX

THIS IS NOT THE INDEX

THIS IS NOT THE INDEX

THIS IS NOT THE INDEX

YOU ARE OFFICIALLY A

Qt π

Qt Creator is CS106B's editor of choice.

I am single and ready to mingle. I enjoy getting roped along into string adventures and can tell you exactly what kind of CHARACTER you're dealing with.

char (aka character)

I am whole(some). I can tell you what the 100th digit of pi is, but I can't return pi to you D-: I love natural numbers and whole ones too!

int (aka integer) or long*

In some ways, I'm an array of characters! You can change some of my character if you want though. I'm pretty popular and often get produced straight from the terminal.

string

True or False, yes or no, I need to know. As a type, I can tell you whether or not something will come to pass. I question everything.

bool (aka boolean)

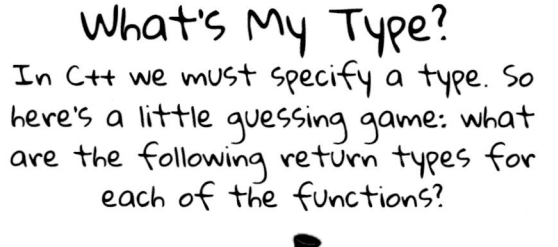

What's My Type?

In C++ we must specify a type. So here's a little guessing game: what are the following return types for each of the functions?

3.14159 babyyyy. I can tell you about rational AND irrational numbers and such. Decimals are my BFF, as they can be real, rational, and irrational with me :)

double or float*

I can do something for you, but I can't return anything to you. Sorry D-:

void

I can give you what some call a list or array of nearly ANY type.

vector

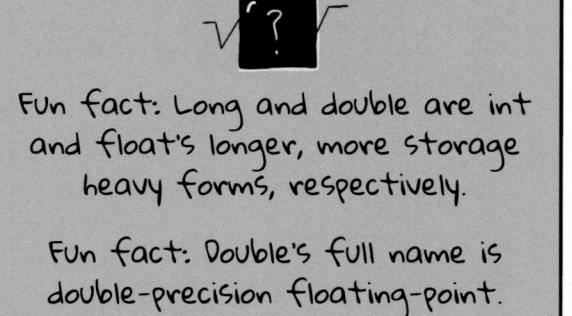

Fun fact: Long and double are int and float's longer, more storage heavy forms, respectively.

Fun fact: Double's full name is double-precision floating-point.

C++ PERSONALITY TEST
WHAT'S YOUR TYPE?

character
char

you are social and love to mix and mingle with other interesting people

boolean
bool

you are very decisive and love to see the beauty in truth; you absolutely hate falsehoods

string
string

you love to surround yourself with interesting characters; you are very versatile and love mixing it up

integer
int

you are very wholesome and love the natural world including nature and numbers

void
void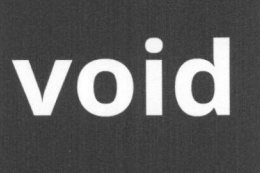

you don't mind ambiguity and do your thing without wondering what people will give in return; very independent

float
float

you have many great, sometimes irrationally complex and drawn out ideas; you love fully expressing yourself and have your head in the clouds

Certificate of Bilingualism

Cs106B student

for now knowing at least 2 CS languages

_____
C++ Camel

Co-Director

_____
Karel Tessier-Lavigne

President

_____
Python Snake

Co-Director

How did the Control Family change in the move from Python to C++? It turns out there were two major changes.

Firstly, every statement/conditional now had parentheses around the expression.

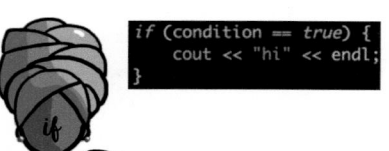

```
if (condition == true) {
    cout << "hi" << endl;
}
```

I just really like parentheses around my statements and brackets to enclose bodies of knowledge.

Modified Mama IF

Secondly, sacred bodies of knowledge were now wrapped in brackets.

```
while (true) {
    //put whatever you need
}
```

Modified Mr. While

For Mama If, elif also turned into else if. Other than that, Mama If and Mr. While pretty much stayed the same.

Here, I prefer things more spelled out!

```
if (x < 5) {
    //do something
}
else if (x < 10) {
    //do something else
}
else {
    //do another thing
}
```

Meet the Control Flow Family– Again
The move to C++

It was Lady For who went through one of the biggest shifts of all, however...

I now want three things in life: initialization, a continuing condition, and incrementation.

```
int n = 10;
//prints numbers from 0 to 9
for (int i = 0; i < n; i++) {
    cout << i << endl;
}
```

This allowed for much variation!

```
//prints out numbers from 1 to 9
for (int i = 1; i <n; i++) {
    cout << i << endl;
}
```

```
//prints numbers from 0 to 10
for (int i = 0; i <= n; i++) {
    cout << i << endl;
}
```

```
//prints out numbers 0, 2, 4, 6, 8
for (int i = 0; i < n; i += 2) {
    cout << i << endl;
}
```

How alike she was to While Loop was even more apparent and allowed for more flexibility.

```
int i = 0;
while (i < n) {
    //do something
    i++;
}
```

```
for (int i = 0; i < n; i++) {
    //do something
}
```

You see, we're just the same!

That you are.

NO, we're not! I'm shorter than you.

And the for each loop was still possible, even if it looked a little bit different as well.

```
Vector<int> nums = {1, 2, 3};
for (int num: nums) {
    cout << num << endl;
}
```

You've got to specify a type once again.

3

Panel 1: Sometimes in function declarations, we'll see the following notation. But what does it mean?

```
void doubleString(string& myString);
```

Did someone reference me?

Panel 2: This is called passing in a variable by REFERENCE. This allows us to modify the variable that is passed in, even after our current function ends.

I work wonders!

I'm the one you're editing the whole time!

```
//doubles the string
void doubleString(string& myString) {
    myString += myString;
}

void testString() {
    string string1 = "hello";
    doubleString(string1);
    //prints "hellohello"
    cout << string1 << endl;
```

Panel 3: By default, variables are passed in by VALUE, meaning that a COPY gets created and used, leaving the original unaffected.

I'm just another variable that happens to have the same value!

```
//we have to return because we can't edit it
string doubleStringValue(string myString) {
    string toReturn = myString + myString;
    return toReturn;
}

void testStringValue() {
    string string1 = "hello";
    string1 = doubleStringValue(string1);
    //prints "hellohello"
    cout << string1 << endl;
```

A clone has been created!

Panel 4: Passing in a variable by REFERENCE—aka passing in the ACTUAL thing—is analogous to someone editing an ORIGINAL Google Doc.

Careful! Anything you do to the original persists outside!

Passing by reference can save space, especially for large variables, as you are not passing in an expensive copy.

Panel 5:

A Tale of
Reference
A story of a Google Doc & change

Panel 6: Passing in a variable by VALUE—aka passing in a COPY—is analogous to a function editing a COPY of the original Google Doc.

I have the same contents, but alas, I'm just a copy! Anything you do to me doesn't affect my original!

We often pass in tinier types (like ints) by value.

Panel 7: Passing in by reference allows for many benefits!

- Saves space by not making expensive copies of variables
- Allows for making changes to variables in functions without having to return
- We can edit multiple variables

Panel 8: One case to look out for is with a for each loop. Here, we also need to make sure we loop through the elements by reference if we wish to change them.

This is like getting the original Google doc but copying each line. The original still isn't edited!

```
Vector<int> nums = {1, 2, 3};
//add & for num to change in nums
for (int& num: nums) {
    num = num*2;
}
```

Panel 9: All in all, reference is a powerful tool that can result in great change!

Cheers to the power of reference!

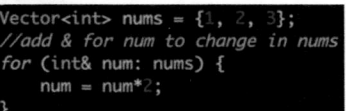

Meet Lady de Bug! The creepy crawly coding bugs hate her because she provides us with tips to help debug them!

After you write a function, test, test, test. Even if you think your code is all right, it's for the best. Thorough testing now means less debugging later, oftentimes this proves to be a lifesaver!

Some recommend running code every 5 to 10 lines, something like that should be just fine.

Double-check logic; double-check intent; this is so easy when you often comment.

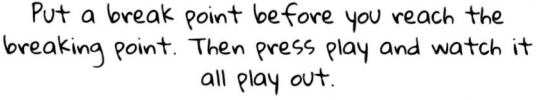
`//commenting is cool :)!`

The debugger is intimidating to befriend but wonderful to be acquainted with.

You're an intimidating stranger but a wonderful friend, you know that :)?

Thanks??

Lessons from Lady de Bug
Sharing tips to help get rid of those pesky C++ bugs

Put a break point before you reach the breaking point. Then press play and watch it all play out.

Put a red dot where you first want things to stop.

```
22  void randomFunction() {
23      //set up a break point!
24  }
```

Take a step in then take a step out to know what your code is all about.

Step into a function to dive into it.

Step over functions you wish to avoid.

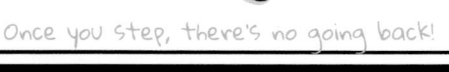
Once you step, there's no going back!

The bug is in the code and thus is bound, but with persistence, grit, and help, it can be found!

Go to LaIR where the SLS care; finish your code or find those bugs with some flair!

Here's a helpful style guide. Good style is great for preventing bugs or making it easier to find them!

With great style you can avoid a pile of bugs in your file!

Take CS106L!
You thought the transition from Python to C++ was hard...
Wait till you see what actual C++ looks like!
TAKE CS106L to learn more about REAL-WORLD C++!!!
Then you'll find out what an ITERATOR is. BWAHAHAHA!!
C++

STYLE AND SYNTAX

Python	C++
# a comment	//a comment
""" a multi-line comment """	/* * a multiline comment */
and, or, not, ==	&& || != ==
True/False	true false

FUNCTIONS AND VARIABLES

Python	C++

# snake case 	
my_function()
my_var = 2
	//camelCase
	int myFunction();
	int myVar = 2;

# var_name = val 	
x = -2
x += 1
x += 5
	int x;
	x = -2;
	x += 1;
	x += 5;

def my_function(x):
    x += 1
    return x
	int myFunction(int x) {
	    x ++;
	    return x;
	}

CONTROL STATEMENTS

Python	C++

if x > 0:
    x += 1
	if (x > 0) {
	    x += 1;
	}

for i in range(2):
    print(i)
	for (int i = 0; i < 2; i++) {
	    cout << i << endl;
	}

for ch in str:
    print(ch)
	for (char ch: str) {
	    cout << ch << endl;
	}

while x < 0:
    x += 1
	while (x < 0) {
	    x += 1;
	}

STRINGS

Python	C++
s = "hi" + " all"	string s = "hi" + "all";
s = "hi all"	string s = "hi all";
s[1] = "p"	s[1] = 'p';
ch = s[1]	char ch = s[1];
len(s)	s.length();
s[len(s) - 1]	s[s.length() - 1];

Python to C++ Scavenger Hunt

SOLUTIONS

STRINGS, PART 2

s[3:] # "all"	s.substr(3); //" all"
s[:3] # "hi "	s.substr(0, 3); //"hi "
s = "abcdefg" s[1:4] # "bcd"	s = "abcdefg"; s.substr(1, 3); // "bcd"
s[a:b]	s.substr(a, b - a);
s[a:]	s.substr(a);
s[:b]	s.substr(0, b);
s[-1]	s.back();

STRINGS, PART 3

Python	C++

index = s.find(substr)
if index != -1:
    print("Found at", index)
	int index = s.find(substr);
	if (index != string::npos) {
	    cout << "Found at " << index;
	}

if substr in s:
    print("Substr is:", substr)
	if (stringContains(s, substr)) {
	    cout << "Substr is: " << substr;
	}

When you're coding in C++, you actually FEEL like a programmer.

Well, when coding in Python, you actually FEEL like a person.

More on transitioning from Python to C++ can be found here!

DATA TYPES

list []	Vector<type> myVector;
dictionary {}	Map<keyType, valueType> myMap;

Chapter Two
LEARNING OUR ADTS
Examining Some C++ Containers

VecTrain the Vector

Griddy

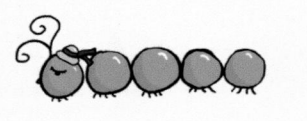

The Queue Caterpillar

Stacks

Set

Ms. Map

YOU GOT THIS!

Fun fact: I was really scared of teaching CS106B, but once I started section-leading it, I ended up becoming a B section leader (SL) for some time. I was also really scared of C++ and CS106B, but once I learned more about it, I came to prefer it to Python. That all is to say, things might be intimidating at first, but once you become more familiar with them, they might become more enjoyable than you ever could have anticipated!

In this chapter, we'll be talking all about Abstract Data Types, or ADTs.

Vector

Grid

Queue

Stack

Set

Map

But what exactly is an ADT?

A D T

An ADT is a coding ABSTRACTION that allows us to use a specific structure without worrying about how exactly it is implemented.

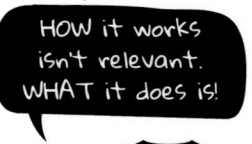

HOW it works isn't relevant. WHAT it does is!

I ♥ ADTS

For example, we might want to store information in a grid. But how do we have a grid to eventually use?

We'll be seeing each other later ;)

What in the world is an ADT?

Although it would be great to try and implement a grid from scratch...

Under the hood, one might use a list of evenly sized rows to represent all the grid data. Each row would be a list with the grid's data type. In C++, lists are called vectors, and so we would implement a vector of vectors. For the user, we'd also have to figure out how to implement expected functions like grid.set(), grid.get(), and grid.in_bounds(). We'd also have to keep track of the number of rows and columns throughout our implementation so that the user can access them at any time. Ideally, we'd also have a resizing function. We'd need to implement these so the person using the grid can use the grid and its functions without worrying about the underlying implementation. If you actually read all of this, congrats! You may be interested in looking at the chapter on classes (chapter 5)! Either way, you'll be learning more about them :0)!

Luckily, we don't have to consider any of that! Someone (in this case, Stanford Uni) has already done that for us!

import "grid.h"

But don't worry, we'll get practice implementing our own ADT soon enough...

And so rather than worry about HOW to implement a grid, we can just use it. We might make a chessboard with a grid of strings or a Boggle board with a grid of chars, for example.

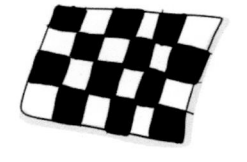

This is with the expectation that the normal grid functions are available to us.

And so, ADTs give us the benefit of cool, useful, ABSTRACTED structures without having to worry about implementation. Yay!

Woohoo!

Meet the first of our ADTs, VecTrain the Vector. An enthusiastic and calm fellow, he can accomodate many elements.

> Welcome to the VecTrain!

Getting déjà vu from VecTrain? This is because Vectors are analogous to Python lists!

Here are a few ways to declare our Vector VecTrain. Vectors from the Stanford library must be declared with a CAPITAL V!

> Only ints allowed on board now!

```
Vector<int> myVec;
Vector<int> myVec = {};
Vector<int> vecTrain = {5, 6, 7};
```

> Choo choo! Welcome aboard 5,6,7 :D

Once VecTrain is set on a type, he cannot change the course. However, VecTrain can be of any type, including Vectors!

> Welcome little Me's!!! Just ma type!

`Vector<Vector<int>> vecTrain`

This is a vector of vectors with integers inside of them.

We can use Vector.size() to get the length of VecTrain.

```
int theSize = vecTrain.size();
```

> I'm three elements long!

Meet the VecTrain the Vector
~ A welcome, orderly, open-minded type of types

We can also index into existing values. Just make sure you have the right type of variable!

```
int thePerfectNum = vecTrain[1];
```

> But remember, accessing an index that doesn't exist means trouble!!!

One can also use vecTrain.get(i) here.

Like a list, we can change values with indexing. To add values, we can use the add() function.

```
vecTrain[1] = 12;
// we CAN'T do this vecTrain[3] = 8
vecTrain.add(8); // CAN do this
```

```
vecTrain[1] = 12;
```

One can also use vecTrain.set(i, value) here.

So how does looping work? Similar to a string, we can do both a for i in range loop. We can also do a for each loop.

```
for (int i = 0; i < vecTrain.size(); i++) {
    int elem = vecTrain[i];
    cout << elem << endl;
}
                    for (int elem: vecTrain) {
                        cout << elem << endl;
                    }
```

> As you see, I'm very orderly.

A vector is ordered. This means it has indexes we can access from first to last.

More on the Stanford vector library can be found here:

Remember Griddy from Python? He's back and with 3 new ways to declare! Just like VecTrain, he now has a specified type when it comes to defining him.

```
Grid<int> griddy;
```

```
Grid<int> griddy2(rows, cols);
Grid<int> griddy3 = {{1, 2, 3}, {4, 5, 6}};
```

Grids consist of different shapes and sizes, defined by their uniform rows and columns. Their rows and columns are also zero-indexed.

Hey, lil' griddy!

```
int numRows = griddy.numRows();
int numCols = griddy.numCols();
```

You can still change any value in Griddy the same way.

```
griddy[row][col] = 0;
```

I am open to change!

We can also use the grid.set(row, col, value) function here.

You can also retrieve and store any value from Griddy in the same way.

```
int zero = griddy[row][col];
```

We can also use the grid.get(row, col) function here.

Meet Griddy Again!
On the block once more

Griddy is flexible, tolerant, and open-minded... until you go out of bounds, that is.

What's the dealio? You are OUT OF BOUNDS with that line! You hear me?

```
int myInt = griddy[row][col]
```

```
int row = 10;
int col = 0;
int badCoord = griddy[row][col];
```

To avoid this tragedy, we have the inBounds function:

```
if (griddy.inBounds(row, col)) {
    //do something!
}
```

It's always good to check boundaries!

To loop through Griddy, we'll often use a nested for loop.

```
for (int row = 0; row < griddy.numRows(); row++) {
    for (int col = 0; col < griddy.numCols(); col++) {
        //prints out all of griddy's coordinates
        cout << row << "," << col << endl;
    }
}
```

One of the coolest tricks in the coding block is looping around!

We can also store specific grid locations in a GridLocation struct, which may prove useful.

```
GridLocation north = {row - 1, col};
GridLocation south = {row + 1, col};
GridLocation east = {row, col + 1};
GridLocation west = {row, col - 1};
```

Meet the Queue Caterpillar, a very special ordered type that acts like a line. Like a line, we can take from the front and add to the back.

```
Queue<int> caterpillar;
Queue<int> qCaterpillar = {6, 1, 2, 3};
```

Why, hello!

However, there is NO indexing. We can only access the front element. We can DEQUEUE it, which stores AND removes it or PEEK— which stores it—WITHOUT removal.

```
qCaterpillar[0] = 0; //a no no      °Type 'Q
qCaterpillar.peek(); //stores last elem
qCaterpillar.dequeue(); //removes last elem
```

INDEXING WILL BREAK ME! Kindly dequeue or peek my first element!

NOTE: If we peek or dequeue an empty queue, we'll have a HUGE ERROR. To avoid this, we'll want to check that the queue isn't empty before calling these functions.

There is NOTHING left to take from me!

```
Queue<int> emptyyy = {};
//ERRORS WILL HAPPEN
emptyyy.peek();
emptyyy.dequeue();
```

As for adding elements, we can only add to the back. We call this enqueueing.

```
qCaterpillar.enqueue(6);
```

I'm not that mysterious. I'm merely a line representation!

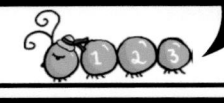

Meet the Queue Caterpillar
Patience, my dear, your turn in line will come.

Naturally, there may be many questions about the Queue Caterpillar. For one, how would we loop through if Queue Caterpillar doesn't have any indexes?

Although some do say I'm a mystery...

We have access to the Queue Caterpillar's size, but this often changes. And if we peek or dequeue an empty queue, we get PROBLEMS. So we can do the following:

```
while (!qCaterpillar.isEmpty()) {
    cout << qCaterpillar.dequeue();
}
```

You've sacrificed my elements to use them!

Thus, the elements accessed first are those that were put in first. Like a line, the Queue Caterpillar is FIFO— first in, first out.

I am FIFO royalty!

More on Queues!

There's how a queue looks like as we dequeue it.

```
//order of dequeuing
// {1, 2, 3, 6}
// {2, 3, 6}
// {3, 6}
// {6}
// {}
```

Take from the front add to the back!

2

Time to learn of a new ADT! This is Stacks! Stacks is basically a pile, while Queue is like a line.

```
Stack<int> myStack;
Stack<int> stacks = {1, 2, 3};
```

Just like Queue, we are unable to access any index. We can remove the top element with the pop() function and also peek.

```
stacks[0] = 0; //a no no        o Type 'Stack<int
stacks.peek(); //stores last elem
stacks.pop(); //removes and stores last elem
```

You can only take from the top of my pile! If you try anything else, I'll fall apart!

We will also get an error if we peek or pop on an empty queue, so we have to do subsequent checks to see if she's empty.

```
Stack<int> emptyStack = {};
//ERRORS WILL HAPPEN
emptyStack.peek();
emptyStack.pop();
```

Make sure I'm not empty!

We can add an element to the top by pushing it onto the stack.

```
stacks.push(4);
```

It's like adding a pancake to a stack!

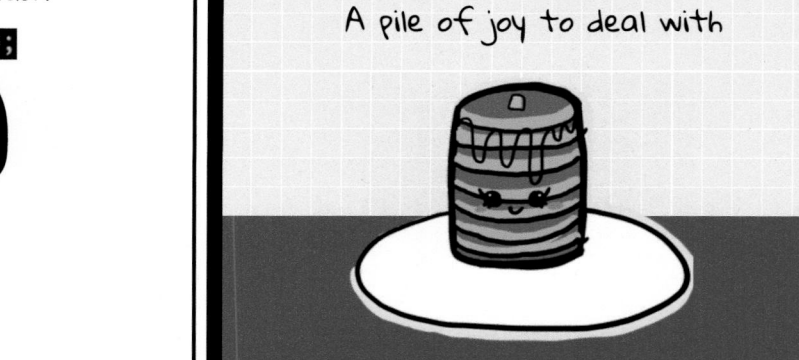

Meet Stacks
A pile of joy to deal with

With both Stacks and Queues, we can also get their size with the size() function.

```
int stackSize = stacks.size();
```

I'm a Stack of all trades!

Looping through is an identical process to the Queue Caterpillar.

```
while (!stacks.isEmpty()) {
    cout << stacks.pop() << endl;
}
```

To create is to destroy!

However, the order of popping and printing is very different.

```
//order of popping
// {1, 2, 3, 4}
// {1, 2, 3}
// {1, 2}
// {1}
// {}
```

In C++, I look like this!

Thus, the elements accessed first are those that were just put in (aka put in last) and stacks is LIFO.

What can I say? I'm full of LIFO!

More on Stacks!

This is Set, another new type who is pretty UNIQUE!

```
Set<int> set;
```

She has NO order at all! She's unordered and unindexed and stores just one of each element, just like a set in math.

```
set[0];
```

> Don't even try to index into me!

You can add elements with the add() function. If an element is already there, nothing changes.

```
set.add(0);
```

> Once you add an element, it's SET for life. Embrace that!

There is a remove() function, though!

If an element is already there, we can check with the contains() function.

```
set.contains(0);
```

> Do I contain the element you're looking for? We shall see!

Meet Set
Every part of her is unique

Here's a common idiom as we often want to do something to an element NOT YET in the set:

```
int elem = 0;
if (!set.contains(elem)) {
    //do something!
    set.add(elem); //now seen
}
```

> If it's not yet contained, let's do something new!

As a set doesn't have an order, how might we go through it? We can use a for each loop here, which goes through every element.

```
for (int elem: set) {
    cout << elem << endl;
}
```

> Alas, you've unlocked the great mystery of how to loop through SET!

With a set, we have some unique operations to generate NEW sets. You may have seen these in math or logic.

```
Set<int> setA = {0, 2, 4, 6, 8, 10};
Set<int> setB = {0, 1, 2, 3, 4, 5};
```

Intersection   Union   Difference

```
Set<int> set;
set = setA.intersect(setB); // {0, 2, 4}
set = setA.unionWith(setB); // {0, 1, 2...10}
set = setA.difference(setB); // {6, 8, 10}
```

We can also use various operators to achieve these operations and more.

```
set = setA + setB; //same as union
set = setA * setB; //same as intersect
set = setA - setB; //same as difference
```

> I do love myself some math as I am born of it :)

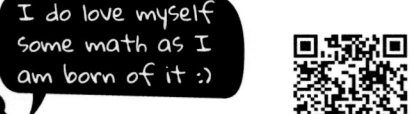

More on Set!

Meet Ms. Map. She is made up of key-value pairs and loves to explore these relationships.

```
Map<string, int> msMap;
msMap = {{"Sierra Leone", 8},
         {"USA", 331},
         {"Australia", 25}};
```

Map of country to population (in millions).

Like dictionaries in Python, we can use her keys to unlock the values. Unlike Python, we can auto-insert entries (e.g., we don't have to check if India is in the map first).

```
msMap["India"] = 1393;
```

C++ automatically generates a "default" type!

Python would throw an error if you did this.

To modify a value, we can access it with the key value and update it.

```
msMap["India"] += 1;
```

Population growth if I ever saw!

Sometimes, the inner value might be another ADT or complex data structure. To handle this, we can access the key[value] and do what we need to do from there.

```
Map<string, Set<char>> msMightyMap;
msMightyMap["VOWELS"].add('a');
```

Did someone say set?

I'm just exploring keys and values, luv!

~ Meet Ms. Map ~
Loving to explore key-value relationships

Sometimes we might even have a nested map!

```
Map<string, Map<string, Vector<string>>> msNested;
msNested["FOODS"]["DESSERTS"].add("PUMPKIN PI");
cout << msNested["FOODS"]["DESSERTS"][0];
```

OUTER KEY   OUTER VALUE

INNER KEY   INNER VALUE

How would we print? We can also use a for each loop here to loop through the keys, and through there, access Ms.Map's values.

```
for (string key: msMap) {
    int value = msMap[key];
    cout << "population of " << key
         << " is " << value << " million!";
}
```

Remember, the keys unlock the values!

Of note is that since maps contain many elements, they often will be passed in by reference!

```
void funWithMsMap(Map<string, int>& msMap) {
    //do something with msMap!
}
```

Ahh, the lovely reference, here to help us save space!

More on Ms. Map can be explored here:

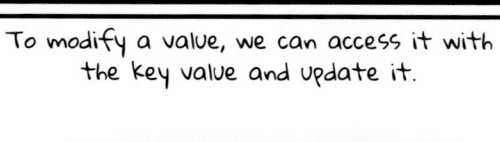

Exploration is the name of the game!

ADT Battle

Would you rather...

Travel on the VecTrain to live in the quiet country

OR

Live in the middle of the grid in the bustling city

Be the first person in a stack

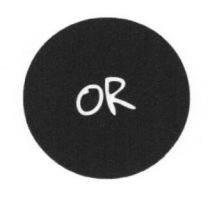

OR

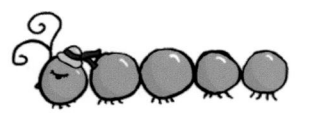

Be the last person in a really long line

Spontaneously pick a random destination from a set of locations to travel to next

OR

Map out your entire journey from start to finish

VECTORS, PART 1

1.
2.
3.

4.

5.

For each of the ADTs, how might we...

1. **IMPORT** the library to use?
2. **DECLARE** the ADT to use?
3. **ITERATE** to add values 1 to 6?
4. **ACCESS** some value to store in an int?
5. **CHANGE** the value at index 2 to 4?
6. **ADD** the value 3?
7. **REMOVE** the value at the end?
8. **PRINT** out the ADT from first/top to last/bottom element?
9. What would the print result be?

Put n/a if something is impossible.

VECTORS, PART 2

6.
7.

8.

9.

STACKS, PART 1

1.
2.
3.

4.

5.

ADT Adventures!

STACKS, PART 2

6.
7.
8.

9.

QUEUES, PART 1

1.
2.
3.

4.

5.

LIBRARIES

Vectors

All libraries

Stacks

Queues

QUEUES, PART 2

6.
7.
8.

9.

SETS, PART 1

1.
2.
3.

4.

SETS, PART 2

5.

6.

7.

For each of the ADTs, how might we...
1. **IMPORT** the library to use?
2. **DECLARE** the ADT to use?
3. **ITERATE** through the whole ADT?
4. **ACCESS** a value to store in a variable?
5. **CHANGE** a value?
6. **ADD** the value 3 (if value/key not added yet?)
7. **PRINT** out the ADT from beginning to end element?

Put n/a if something is impossible.

MAPS, PART 1

1.
2.
3.

4.

MAPS, PART 2

5.

6.

7.

ADT Adventures!

GRIDS, PART 1

1.
2.
3.

4.

GRIDS, PART 2

5.

6.

7.

Sets   *Maps*

LIBRARIES

Grids   *Grid Locs*

VECTORS, PART 1

```
1. #include "vector.h"

2. Vector<int> myVec;

3. for (int i = 0; i <= 6; i++) {
          myVec.add(i);
   }

4. int myInt = myVec[j]; // j is index

5. myVec[2] = 4;
```

For each of the ADTs, how might we...
1. **IMPORT** the library to use?
2. **DECLARE** the ADT to use?
3. **ITERATE** to add values 1 to 6?
4. **ACCESS** some value to store in an int?
5. **CHANGE** the value at index 2 to 4?
6. **ADD** the value 3?
7. **REMOVE** the value at the end?
8. **PRINT** out the ADT from first/top to last/bottom element?
9. What would the print result be?

Put n/a if something is impossible.

VECTORS, PART 2

```
6. myVec.add(3);

7. myVec.remove(myVec.length() - 1);

8. for(int i=0; i < myVec.size();i ++){
          cout << myVec[i];
   }

9. {1, 2, 4, 4, 5, 6}
```

STACKS, PART 1

```
1. #include "stack.h"

2. Stack<int> myStack;

3. for (int i = 0; i <= 6; i++) {
          myStack.push(i);
   }

4. int myInt = myStack.peek();

5. can't do, can only access last value
```

ADT Adventures!
Potential Solution

STACKS, PART 2

```
6. myStack.push(3)

7. myStack.pop()

8. while (!myStack.isEmpty()) {
          cout << myStack.pop();
   }

9. {6, 5, 4, 3, 2, 1}
```

QUEUES, PART 1

```
1. #include "queue.h"

2. Queue<int> myQueue;

3. 3. for (int i = 0; i <= 6; i++) {
          myQueue.enqueue(i);
   }

4. int myInt = myQueue.peek();

5. can't do, can only access latest value
```

Vectors   *All libraries*

LIBRARIES

Stacks   *Queues*

QUEUES, PART 2

```
6. myQueue.enqueue(3);

7. myQueue.dequeue();

8. while (!myStack.isEmpty()) {
          cout << myQueue.dequeue();
   }

9. {1, 2, 3, 4, 5, 6}
```

SETS, PART 1

```
1. #include "set.h"

2. Set<int> mySet;

3. for (int elem: mySet) {

   }
   // no indexing!

4. if (mySet.contains(value)) {
       int myInt = value;
   }
```

For each of the ADTs, how might we...
1. **IMPORT** the library to use?
2. **DECLARE** the ADT to use?
3. **ITERATE** through the whole ADT?
4. **ACCESS** a value to store in a variable?
5. **CHANGE** a value?
6. **ADD** the value 3 (if value/key not added yet?)
7. **PRINT** out the ADT from beginning to end element?

Put n/a if something is impossible.

SETS, PART 2

```
5. not directly possible


6. if (!mySet.contains(3)) {
       set.add(3);
}


7. for (int elem: mySet) {
       cout << elem;
}
```

MAPS, PART 1

```
1. #include "map.h"

2. Map<string, int> myMap;

3. for (string key: myMap.keys()) {
       value = myMap[value];

   }

4. int myInt = myMap[key];
```

ADT Adventures!
Potential Solution

MAPS, PART 2

```
5. myMap[key] = value;


6. if (!myMap.contains(key)) {
       myMap[key] = value;
   }


7. for (string key: myMap.keys()) {
       cout << key << ":" <<
            myMap[key];
}
```

GRIDS, PART 1

```
1. #include "grid.h"

2. Grid<int> myGrid(row, col);

3. for (int row = 0; row <
       myGrid.numRows(); i++) {
     for (int col = 0; col <
       myGrid.numCols(); i++) {

     }
}

4. int myInt = myGrid[row][col];
```

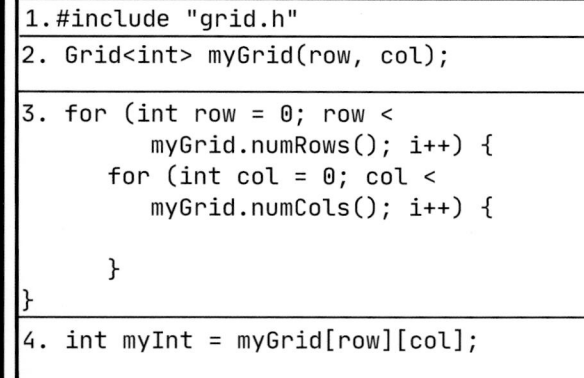

Sets

Maps

LIBRARIES

Grids

Grid Locs

GRIDS, PART 2

```
5. myGrid[row][col] = value

6. //not really applicable

7. for (int row = 0; row <
       myGrid.numRows(); i++) {
       for (int col = 0; col <
           myGrid.numCols(); i++) {
           cout<< grid[row][col];
       }
}
```

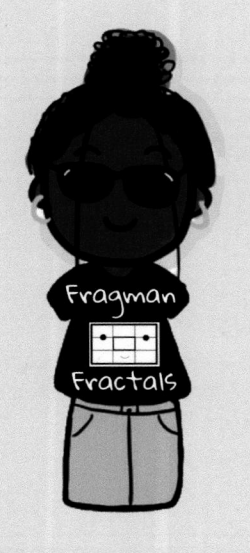

Chapter Three
BIG-O, RECURSION, AND BACKTRACKING

Big-O

Recursia

The Backtracker

Big-O can be really big! Unbeknownst to him, everybody wants to REDUCE his large presence. But there is only so much they can do.

What do you mean ONLY O(n)?

But who is Big-O? He's a company executive obsessed with runtime complexity, that is, how long the function takes to run as the input size grows, all the way until infinity!

And I mean business. Longer runtime means less effiecient means LESS MONEY!

I don't think he realizes HE is the problem.

Since runtime is very different on every device, Big-O is very concerned with the number of steps taken as a measure of time. But what does that mean?

I charge one unit of time per print service job.

To illustrate, let's use worker n as input.

In a perfect world, no matter the input size, the number of steps would remain the same. This is called O(1), or CONSTANT Big-O runtime.

No matter how much I grow, the work/steps will be constant and stay the same. So efficient!

Meet Big-O
A mean, not-so lean company executive concerned only with growth

This can be demonstrated with a scenario where we print out the total number of workers.

Whether I represent one worker or a thousand workers, there is just one step—the print step— every time!

```
void printNumWorkers(int n) {
    cout << n << endl;
}
```

But oftentimes, the input size does affect how long/how many steps we take. What if we print out the worker ID for each worker?

If there is one worker, I do one print job. But if there are a million workers... Welp!

```
void printWorkerId(int n) {
    for (int i = 0; i < n; i++) {
        cout << i << endl;
    }
}
```

This is known as O(n) or LINEAR runtime. As our input size increases, the number of steps increases by a linear factor.

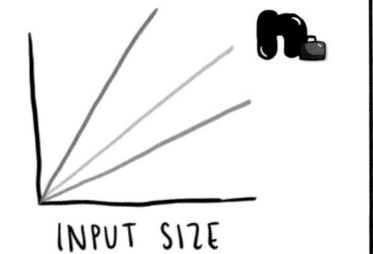

RUNTIME/ STEPS

INPUT SIZE

Charts can be super duper helpful in illustrating this. We can put our computer runtime to approximate it.

O(1)	
n	runtime
1	1 sec
2	1 sec
3	1 sec
1000	1 sec

O(n)	
n	runtime
1	1 sec
2	2 sec
3	3 sec
1000	1000 sec

What about variations in constant time and linear time?

You know I'm charging double for print jobs now?

```
O(1)
n       runtime
1       2 sec
2       2 sec
3       2 sec
1000    2 sec
It's 2 units now
```

```
void printNumWorkers(int n) {
    cout << n << endl;
    cout << "welcome to work!" << endl;
}
```

It turns out that Big-O doesn't care about those.

I don't care. It's the big picture that matters, the long run. As far as I'm concerned, you're constant! Whether it's a constant 5 secs or 10, doesn't matter!

Big-O only cares about the largest term and its growth. No coefficients. No smaller terms.

$5n^2 + n - 10$ is still $O(n^2)$.

It's true... all I care about is long-term growth!

Let's further examine some common cases, starting with O(n).

Often times, I'm just a for loop, but O(n) can be surprisingly deceptive!

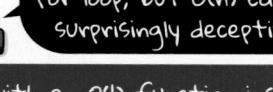

- For loop with an O(1) function inside
  - for (int i = 3; i < n - 4; i += 10) works
  - for (int i = 0; i < 100) DOES NOT!
- Successive O(n) functions are still O(n)
- When you have to go over each element in a collection, that's O(n) behavior

---

Meet Big-O
Taking a closer look at all the work behind the scenes

Be careful, though, not all functions inside for loops are O(1)!

O(1) functions
- enqueue/dequeue
- push/pop
- peek
- size
- add/index (vector)
- print/cout

O(n) functions
- insert (vector)
- remove (vector)
- sublist (vector)
- clear (map/set)
- mapAll

If an O(n) function is INSIDE a for loop that's O(n), Big-O is O(n^2).

O(n^2) is also known quadratic behavior.

I scale fast!

- Nested O(n) for loops (grids, 2D objects)
- One O(n) for loop with an O(n) function inside
- The box method: Draw a box around the content in a for loop and the for loop itself; then, multiply their Big-Os together to get the total Big-O

O(log n) is also known as logarithmic runtime.

I tend to happen when you can cut things in half (like the number of elements to search) each iteration!

O(log n) functions
- add (set)
- contains (set)
- remove (map/set)
- put/get (map)
- containsKey (map)
- indexing (map)

NOTE: O(log n) is FASTER than O(n)

Good luck working with Big-O!

FUN FACT: Big-O's O represents Ordnung!

RECURSION AHEAD

RECURSION AHEAD

RECURSION AHEAD

RECURSION AHEAD

RECURSION AHEAD

RECURSION AHEAD

If you or a friend is struggling through recursion, go to LaIR. More information available at cs106b.stanford.edu

So you've heard of functions calling helper functions...

I need help!

soundex()

I'm here to help!

encodeString()

But have you heard of functions calling themselves?

I need help!

doFactorial()

I'm here to help!

doFactorial()

This is called recursion. Recursia is here to help us understand that! She's an interesting soul, interested in fractals, self-similarity, and pattern-thinkng.

Recursia to the rescue :)!

Recursion is a topic that pops up in nature.

shells

snowflakes

galaxies

trees

Meet Recursia
In order to meet Recursia, you need to meet Recursia

So... if a function is ALWAYS calling itself, how do we stop it? Shouldn't it be infinite?

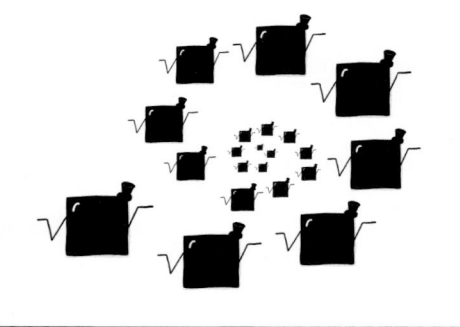

That's why we have something called a base case! After Recursia is done branching out, there lies something called a base case, the key to STOPPING everything.

Recursia loves apples!

It's one of the few times a recursive function returns something that isn't calling itself. The base case returns its value to the function that called it.

A less mind-boggling gift to return!

In the recursive case, however, we do call the function over and over and over again. This is called a recursive call.

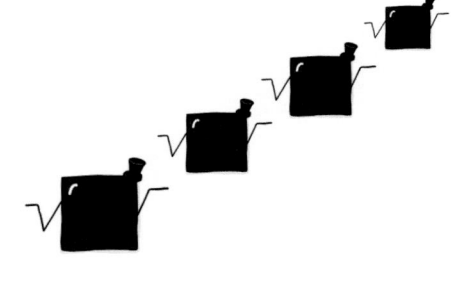

Let's look at a recursive implementation of a factorial function to examine things.

```
int doFactorial(int n) {
    if (n == 0) {
        return 1;
    }
    return n*doFactorial(n - 1);
}
```

I'm a recursive function, I feature in my own function :)

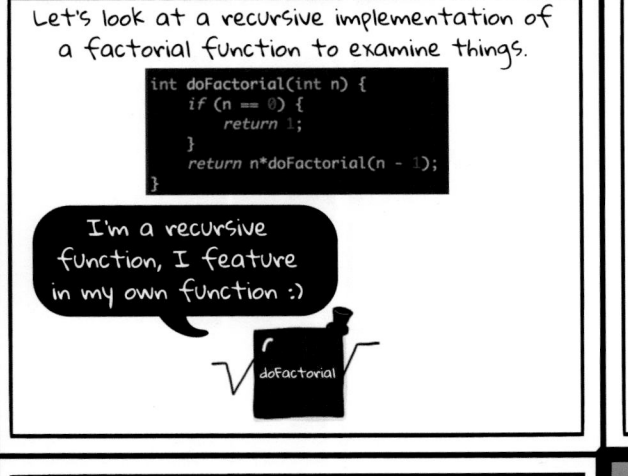

As a reminder, a factorial is done when we take a number and multiply it by all the positive numbers up to that number.

So 3! is 3 * 2 * 1 = 6, and 5 factorial is 5 * 4 * 3 * 2 * 1 = 120.

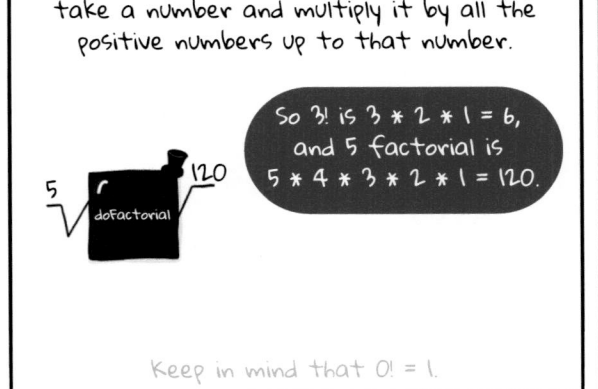

Keep in mind that 0! = 1.

Notice any patterns?

0! = 1
1! = 1
2! = 2
3! = 6
4! = 24
5! = 120

Hint: What's the relationship between the previous and current factorial of a number?

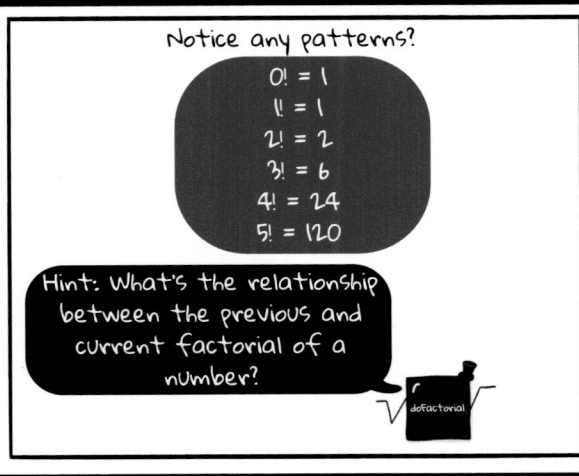

There is a self-similarity that presents itself. What if, when solving a factorial, we had a function that automatically calculated the factorial of 1 number less?

Oh! If only someone could help me with 4 factorial! Work would be easier....

Well, I've got news for you!

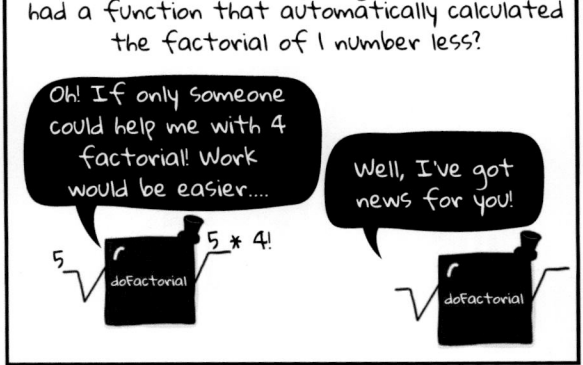

Meet Recursia
Examining Factorial

Then we could just do n*doFactorial(n - 1), generated from the helper function. And we do have that function!

Surprise! I'm here to help!

So in this case, our recursive case would be n times the factorial of (n - 1). We know how to return that.

Sounds like a recursive call to me!

Remember that the recursive call happens when the function calls itself.

But how do we know when to stop returning in a recursive function? This is where our base case comes in! Once we hit the case where n is 0, we know to stop.

I have something other than myself to return to you :)!

Sounds like a base case to me!

Each function calls a recursive helper. This stops when we hit the base case. From there, each function returns its value to the function that CALLED it and then finishes.

With recursion, the first thing we often want to think about is a base case. 1) What do we RETURN as an actual VALUE, and 2) What is the SIMPLEST possible case?

What's the SIMPLEST possible input such that we can return an actual value rather than do another recursive call?

Base Case   Recursive Call

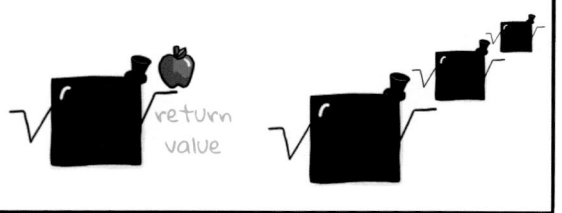
return value

Trying to find the simplest possible case might just surprise you. These are often simpler than the general use cases for the function.

SOME SIMPLE INPUTS
- An empty vector/string
- A vector/string with one element
- The integer 0

Sometimes, it's not a matter of the simplest common case but a finished input such that it makes sense to stop.

SOME FINISHED INPUTS
- An index equal to the size of a vector
- A string of a full/desired length
- A condition that has been satisfied

Meet Recursia
More on Base Cases

In addition to the base condition, we also need to figure out WHAT to RETURN.

If it's a boolean, we need to figure out the true and false conditions.

If it's an int, what number are we returning?

Always remember the type of what you're returning because ultimately the base case and recursive call return that type.

Even if it takes a long time, I still have to return a certain type!

Sometimes, the return is void, and instead of returning a value, we add to a list or set or draw something. With void functions, if we hit a base case we can just return.

Sometimes I perform a task recursively and it has NO return value. It's VOIDDD!

Recursion is so versatile!

And remember that having a base case is the key to stopping recursion from going on forever.

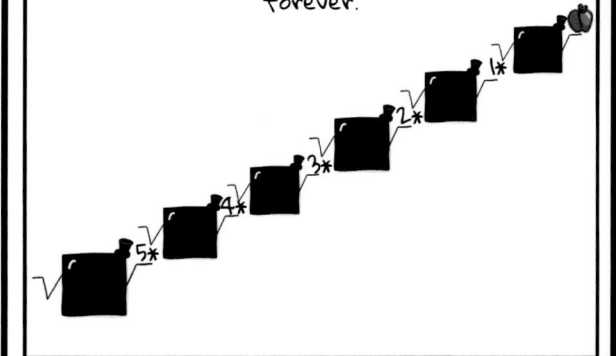

Now let's look a little bit more at recursive cases.

Somehow, the recursive function has to be the same function but take in an input that takes us closer to the base case.

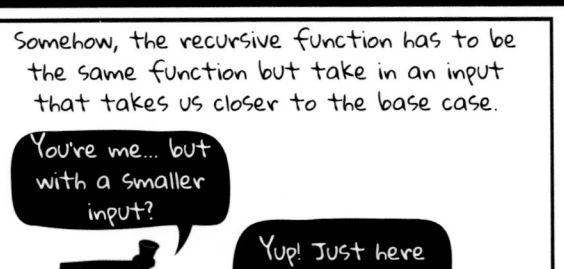

You're me... but with a smaller input?

Yup! Just here to assist!

And eventually, it gets close enough to reach the base case. We just take a recursive LEAP of FAITH and hope it all works.

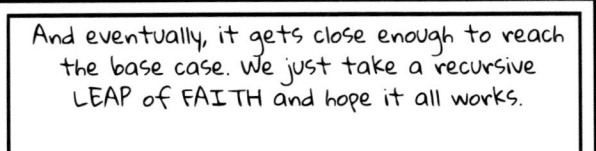

I trust that one day, we'll get there.

Remember that with recursion, you are using a helper function; the helper function just happens to be ANOTHER call to the SAME function.

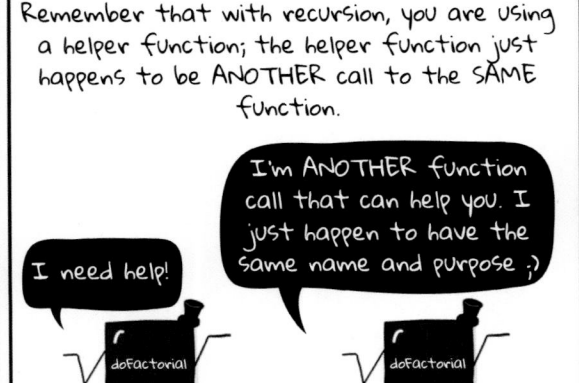

I need help!

I'm ANOTHER function call that can help you. I just happen to have the same name and purpose ;)

Meet Recursia
More on Recursive Cases

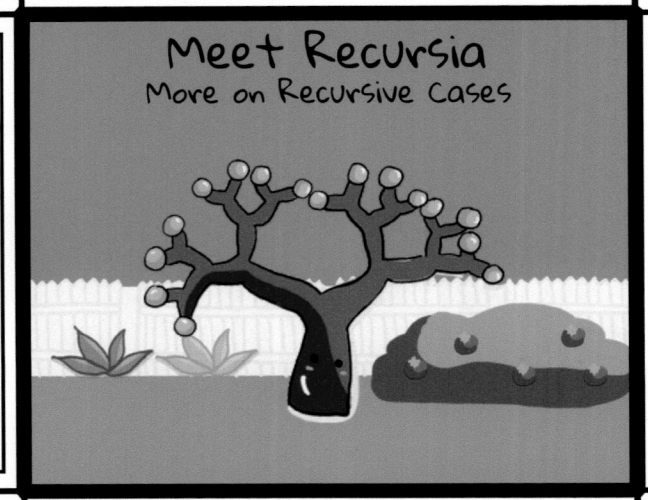

So how might we snip things down to eventually get to the base case?

We might increment an integer to a certain point or decrement it like in factorial.

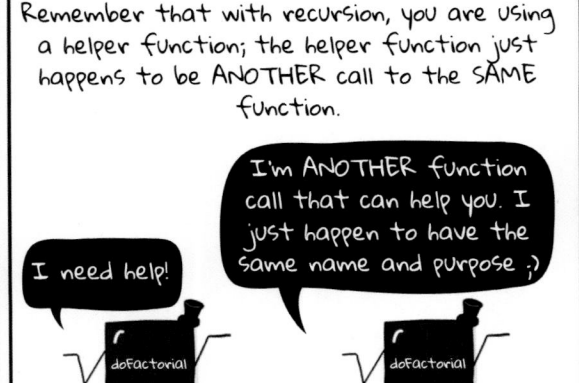

We might break down a string or build another string up.

Note: Be careful with s.erase() and s.substring functions. s.erase() modifies the string!

We might break it down to a certain condition.

Looks like we made it to the starting coordinate! That means we've found a path!

int numberInLine(Queue<string> line);

The goal of this function is to find the number of people waiting in a line **using recursion**. No loops allowed. It takes in a queue of strings representing people in a line and returns the number of people in the line.

bool isPalindrome(string word);

The goal of this function is to find out whether a certain word is a palindrome, meaning that it is the same forwards and backwards.

int findFactorial(int n);

The goal of this function is to calculate n! using recursion.

void genSubLists(Vector<int> numberSet, Vector<Vector<int>>& allSubLists);

The goal of this function is to generate a list made up of all the possible sublists of a vector.

Hint: Use a helper wrapper function here!

Recursion Excursion

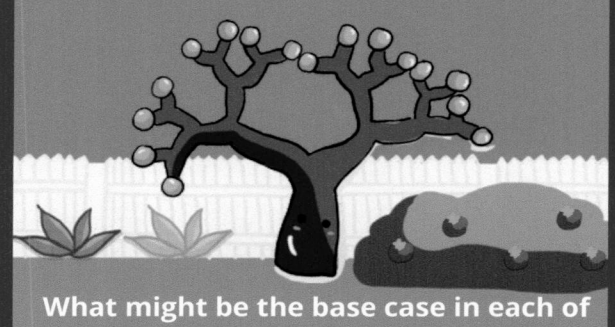

What might be the base case in each of the following?

void drawFractalGrid(int order);

The goal of this function is to draw a Fractal Grid of order n.

Note: A creative exercise!

Pitfalls
- Making base cases too extensive
- Trying to handle a base case in the recursive case
- Base case doesn't actually signify end of function
- Base case isn't reached because of how recursive case is set up

Recursion is so cool!

Ease of Understanding

Elegance!

Clean code

General tips
- Think of the tiniest possible input that can be put into the function WITHOUT thinking about recursion. If we wanted to see if a word was a palindrome, what might the tiniest input be?
- Oftentimes, the base case is an edge case.
- Ask yourself, when might we want to stop?

int numberInLine(Queue<string> line);

The goal of this function is to find the number of people waiting in a line **using recursion**. No loops allowed. It takes in a queue of strings representing people in a line and returns the number of people in the line.

bool isPalindrome(string word);

The goal of this function is to find out whether a certain word is a palindrome, meaning that it is the same forwards and backwards.

int findFactorial(int n);

The goal of this function is to calculate n! using recursion.

void genSubLists(Vector<int> numberSet, Vector<Vector<int>>& allSubLists);

The goal of this function is to generate a list made up of all the possible sublists of a vector.

Hint: Use a helper wrapper function here!

Recursion Excursion

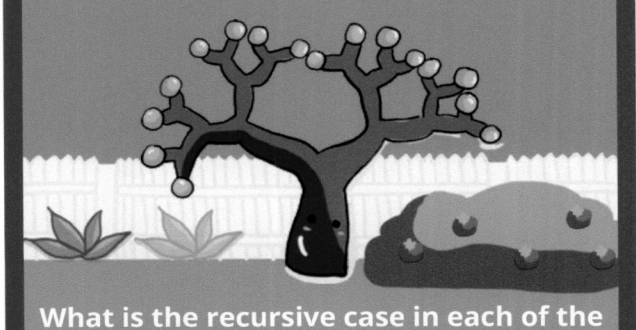

What is the recursive case in each of the following?

void drawFractalGrid(int order);

The goal of this function is to draw a Fractal Grid of order n.

Note: A creative exercise!

Pitfalls
- The recursive case doesn't lead to the base case
  - Ex. *Your base case depends on a string being empty, but you never erase parts of the string.*
- Mistakenly modifying something at every level of recursion
- Not including additional parameters

But there are still pitfalls!
Too many calls on the call stack could result in Stack Overflow!!!!!

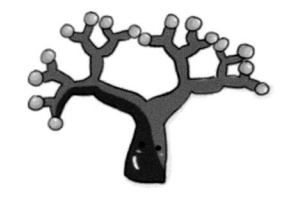

There's something called Unrolling the recursion :)

General tips
- Imagine that the recursive call ISN'T recursive but rather a helper function that MAGICALLY helps you to solve the problem (alternatively, you can think of it as the same function, but somehow implemented iteratively).
- DRAW IT OUT with a very simple test case.
- DRAW the stack out as well, with each function represented as a box.

Sometimes, instead of getting a single solution, we want to generate a POOL of possibilities to choose from. The Backtracker is here to help us with that!

We use backtracking in 3 main ways.

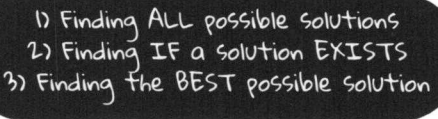

1) Finding ALL possible solutions
2) Finding IF a solution EXISTS
3) Finding the BEST possible solution

No matter which way you choose, you have to generate all possible solutions. Do you see why, my dudes?

Approach 1 does this naturally. For approach 2, you begin generating but may stop. For approach 3, we need to know all possibilities.

With backtracking, it's best to DRAW THINGS OUT! Let's look at an example where the goal is to find and print all possible n-letter words given a word of n letters.

eta -> {"eta", "eat", "tea", "ate"}

Recursion is what helps us to generate all these possibilities.

Meet the Backtracker!
Finding fun ways to explore the solution space.

The first step is to draw a decision tree of all possibilities.

"" so far
(eta) remaining

"e"
(ta)

"t"
(ea)

"a"
(et)

"et"
(a)

"ea"
(t)

"tc"
(a)

"ta"
(e)

"ae"
(t)

"at"
(e)

"eta"   "eat"   "tea"   "tae"   "aet"   "ate"

One type of tree decides WHICH option to choose. This usually results in a for loop with each iteration trying a different option.

```
// remains[i] is each letter
for (int i = 0; i < remains.length(); i++) {
```

When you're deciding WHICH element to use, you can use a for loop where you try each option out!

Let's look at an example where our tree decides to PICK or SKIP an option. This example deals with generating all subsets.

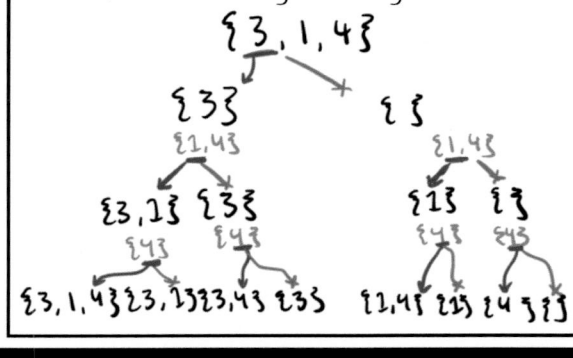

For these problems, instead of a for loop, we have two recursive options, one that PICKS the option and one that skips it.

```
genSubListsHelper(numberList, index + 1, currSubList, allSubLists);
Vector<int> newList = currSubList;
newList.add(numberList[index]);
genSubListsHelper(numberList, index + 1, newList, allSubLists);
```

First option skips, second option picks.

To pick or to skip; that is the question.

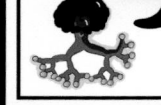

One paradigm to explore an option is to CHOOSE temporary inputs, recursively EXPLORE the option, and then UNCHOOSE those inputs.

We have to leave the room like how we met it for the next option.

For example, we want to independently explore "e" and "t". When we explore e though, soFar becomes "e". But we have to reset it to "" when we explore "t."

Some patterns are the following:

soFar:
choose a character
explore recursion
Unchoose char

remaining:
remove a character
explore recursion
insert char

```
for (int i = 0; i < remains.length(); i++) {
    //choose step
    soFar += remains[i]; // "" -> "e"
    string ogRemains = remains; //store for later
    remains.erase(i, 1); // "eta" -> "ta"
    //explore step
    genWordsHelper(remains, soFar); //explore
    //unchoose after we've explored
    soFar.erase(soFar.length() - 1); //"e"-> ""
    remains = ogRemains; // "ta" -> "eta"
}
```

WATCH OUR FOR S.SUBSTR() VS S.ERASE()!

The base case occurs with a solution or when we can't go any further. We can also prune when a possibility will yield an invalid solution.

Some patterns
- Index is >= len
- soFar is full
- remaining is empty

```
if (isWord(soFar)) { //a
    cout << soFar << end
}
if (remains.empty()) {
    return;
}
```

```
if (isPrefixDNE(soFar)) {
    return;
}
```

```
if (index == numberList.size()) {
    allSubLists.add(currSubList);
    return;
}
```

Note: DNE means does not exist

Assume isWord() and isPrefixDNE() exist!

Sometimes, we'll have a solution but want to keep exploring. An example is if we were trying to find ALL words, not just 3-letter ones.

```
if (isWord(soFar)) { //assume this fn exists
    cout << soFar << endl;
}
```

Just keep searching!

Meet the Backtracker!
Finding fun ways to explore the solution space

From then on, there are some differences in the three approaches. For finding all solutions, once we find all solutions, we usually add it to some collection.

Another apple to add!

This might be a set, list, or involve printing.

For finding a potential solution, we usually want to return early in the base and/or recursive case once we've found a solution.

I've found the apple of my eye!

```
//in base case
//if found solution
//      return true
//in recursive case
// for letter in letters
//      ...
//      if (recursionWord()) {
//          return true
//      ...
// return false
```

For finding the best solution, we often compare and update the best option in the base case or recursive case until we've gone through all possibilities.

```
//for letter in letters
//     ....
//     curr = recursiveCall()
//     if (curr > best)
//         best = curr
//     ...
// return best
```

The best apple has truly been found!

Sometimes, the paramters passed in aren't enough for what we need. This is where recursive wrapper helper functions come in!

```
void genWords(string word) {
    genWordsHelper(word, "");
}
```

Sometimes backtracking requires a little extra pizzaz!

For example, we may need to keep track of soFar and remaining, but only receive a word.

4

```cpp
int numberInLine(Queue<string> line) {
    if (line.isEmpty()) {
        return 0;
    }
    line.dequeue();
    return 1 + numberInLine(line)
}
```

```cpp
bool isPalindrome(string word) {
    if(word.empty()) {
        return true;
    }
    else if (word.size() == 1) {
        return true;
    }
    else {
        if (word[0] == word[word.length() - 1]) {
            string sub = word.substr(1, word.length() - 2);
            return isPalindrome(sub);
        }
    }
    return false;
}
```

```cpp
int findFactorial(int n) {
    if (n == 0) {
        return 1;
    }
    return n*findFactorial(n -1);
}
```

```cpp
void genSubListsHelper(Vector<int> numberList,
                       int index, Vector<int> currSubList,
                       Vector<Vector<int>>& allSubLists) {
    if (index == numberList.size()) {
        allSubLists.add(currSubList);
        return;
    }
    genSubListsHelper(numberList, index + 1, currSubList, allSubLists);
    currSubList.add(numberList[index]);
    genSubListsHelper(numberList, index + 1, currSubList, allSubLists);
    currSubList.remove(numberList[index]);
}

void genSubLists(Vector<int> numberSet,
                 Vector<Vector<int>>& allSubLists) {
    genSubListsHelper(numberSet, 0, {}, allSubLists);
}
```

Recursion Excursion

Soln

This one is for you to figure out in your own way :)

Fragman, Fractal Gridding mascot

Chapter Four
MAKING MEMORIES
. . . with Pointers, Heaps, Call Stacks, and Structs

The Memory Palace

Mr. Pointer

Stone Mason Struct

C. Stack

The Heap

New

Delete

Fun fact: Variables don't just exist in a vacuum.

We don't?

They actually live somewhere, and that somewhere is C++'s memory— what we'll call the Memory Palace!

I am a house with an actual home address!

123 STACK STREET

Home

SIDE NOTE: Although there's a distinction between virtual and physical memory, for now that doesn't matter. So you can think of memory as a physical place!

PRETEND I'M AN ACTUAL PHYSICAL PLACE FOR SIMPLICITY!

This Memory Palace is where everything is stored, and we'll be focusing on where variables live and are stored.

Welcome to the Memory Palace
Storing memory in computer space

Each variable actually has its own address, represented by a hexadecimal value. So if you see something like 0xa12345, that's probably a memory address of something!

Address 0x123 That's where I live!

0x123 Stack St.

For more on hexadecimal, go to page 33 of the CS106A side.

A variable's memory address is very precious, for if you know it, you have access to its soul! You can modify the variable itself without needing to pass it in by reference.

Oh gosh! Now they know where I live!!

lurks

In this next section, we'll be exploring how we can access this memory and manipulate it. We'll be answering questions such as...

When a variable goes out of scope, where does it go?

Can a variable exist beyond the scope of its function (Can it break out of the black box)?

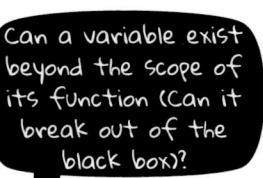

And we'll meet a slew of new characters who all inhabit and have special access to different parts of the Memory Palace.

We can access the memory address of a variable with the following notation.

```
&x; //gets address 0x123 of variable x
```

This notation isn't seen much in CS106B. It is "overloaded" as the reference sign, however.

This retrieves the address of the variable from memory.

But what is the variable type that contains this address?

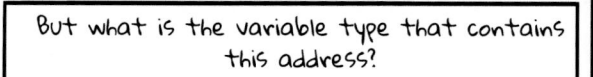

It's time to meet Mr. Ptr, a new variable type called a pointer! A pointer IS JUST A NUMBER that represents a memory address. It's declared like so:

```
int* mrPtr = &x;
```

Meet Mr. Ptr
Under the surface, just a memory address

We say that a pointer POINTS to the variable whose address it has.

We declare Mr. Ptr by adding a star to an existing data type because we need to know WHAT kind of variable he's pointing to.

```
int x = 10;
int* mrIntPtr = &x;

string hi = "hello";
string* mrStringPtr = &hi;
```

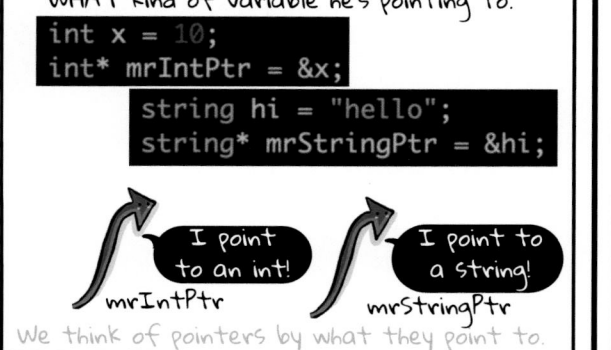

We think of pointers by what they point to.

At the end of the day, Mr. Ptr is just a variable. He just happens to be a variable that "points to" another variable.

```
int x = 10;
int* mrIntPtr = &x;
```

As Lecturer Chris often says, a pointer is just a number representing a memory address!

Pointers like Mr. Ptr allow us to access the address of a variable, its soul, and therefore modify a variable in new ways.

```
int x = 10;
int* mrIntPtr = &x;
```

1

Remember: Having a variable's address lends us access to its soul. When we DEREFERENCE a pointer, we have access to the variable itself!

```
// *(mrPtr) retrieves x
int num = *(mrPtr); //num = x
```

I've conjured up the variable I point to!

0x123 Stack St.

The * is overloaded. It represents both pointer declaration and dereferencing.

Through dereferencing a pointer, we can also change its variable's value PERMANENTLY.

```
// this CHANGES x to 10
*(mrPtr) = 10;
```

I've been modified!!!

0x123 Stack St.

Sometimes, Mr. Ptr is POINTING to NOTHING. If Mr. Ptr is nullptr, that means he's not pointing to any address.

```
int* mrNullPtr = nullptr;
```

I feel... pointless!

0x0

0x0 is not an actual address but rather a placeholder value for nothing.

Be careful! If you dereference a nullptr, you will see errors you never knew existed.

```
int* mrNullPtr = nullptr;
*(mrNullPtr) = 10; //HUGE ERROR
```

You'll find out soon enough....

What is a segfault?

0x0

Befriending Mr. Ptr
Some more pointers on pointers

So, when you are dereferencing Mr. Ptr in any form, remember to check whether he is null.

```
int* mrPtr = nullptr;
if (mrPtr == nullptr) {
    return; //it's for the best!
}
```

It's probably my fault if you get a segfault!

0x0

So all in all, pointers allow us to access a variable and modify it without having to deal with the variable directly.

Once you have my address, you can do anything you want with me :(Scary!

0x123 Stack St.

Note the difference between the value a pointer is POINTING to and the pointer's value itself (the address).

I'm pointing to a value of 10, but I myself am 0x123.

0x123

With great power comes great responsbility!

Pointer power!

What does it mean, then, to set to pointers equal to each other? Just like any variable, they now have the same value.

```
int* mrsPtr = mrPtr;
```

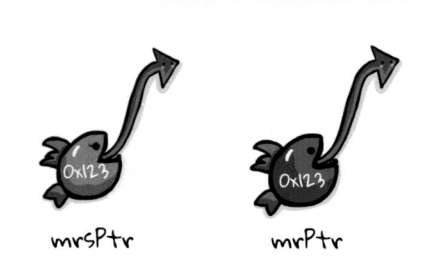

This means that they are now POINTING to the SAME THING. So when we reassign a pointer, it now points to something new.

```
int* mrsPtr = mrPtr;
```

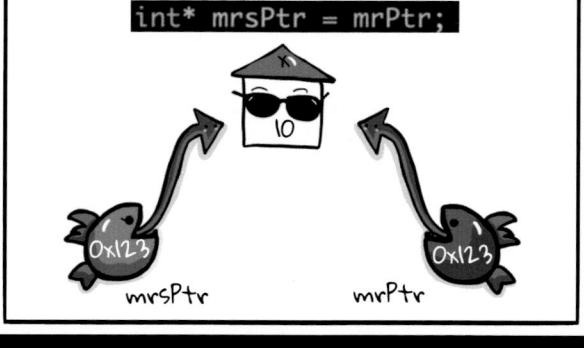

When two things point to the same thing, modifying the variable through one pointer modifies that for both pointers.

```
*(mrsPtr) = 23;
cout << *(mrPtr); //couts 23 as well
```

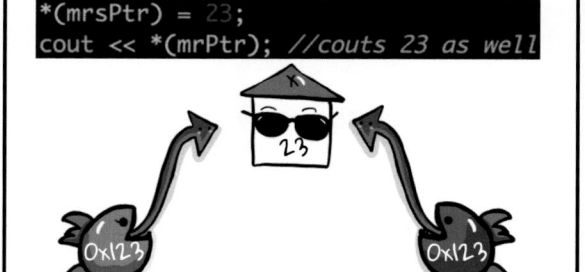

In general, if we change the value of the pointer itself, that changes where it points to.

```
int y = 19;
mrPtr = &(y);
```

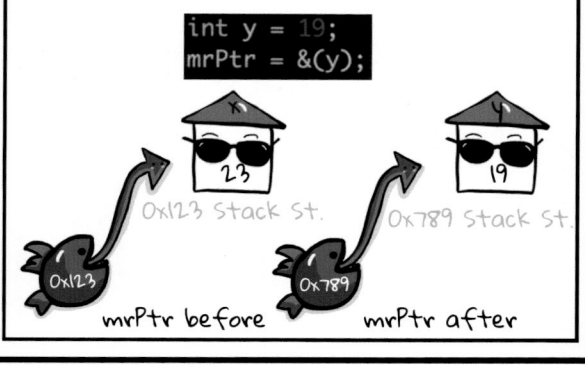

0x123 Stack St.   0x789 Stack St.

mrPtr before   mrPtr after

Befriending Mr. Ptr
Pointing us in the right direction

I change DIRECTION when the pointer value is reassigned.

Often, pointers make it so that we don't need to pass in a variable by reference; rather, we can pass in its pointer.

Before
```
void modifyVar(int& x);
```
After
```
void modifyVarWithPtr(int* mrPtr);
```

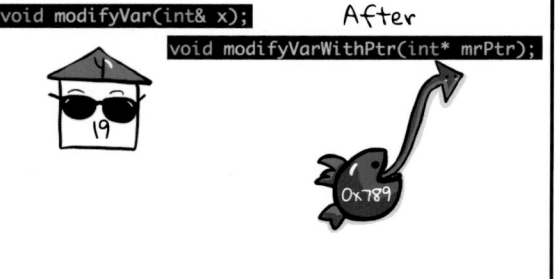

However, if we're changing the pointer value itself within a function, this means we'll want to pass it the pointer by reference.

```
void modifyPtr(int*& mrPtr);
```

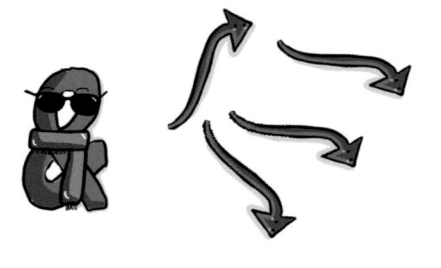

Remember that at the end of the day, a pointer is just a number that represents a memory address, despite how we abstract it!

Each time we call a function, it opens its own place in the Memory Palace called a stack frame. All stack frames lie on the Call Stack. Call Stack likes to go by C. Stack.

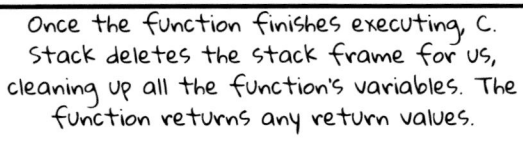

I'm C. Stack!

Each stack frame on C. Stack controls all the variables held within that function. Often, this starts with the parameters, since they are passed in by value, meaning a copy of them is made.

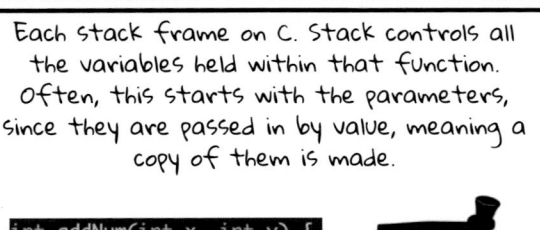

```
int addNum(int x, int y) {
    return x + y;
}
```

addNum()

- x
- y

Once the function finishes executing, C. Stack deletes the stack frame for us, cleaning up all the function's variables. The function returns any return values.

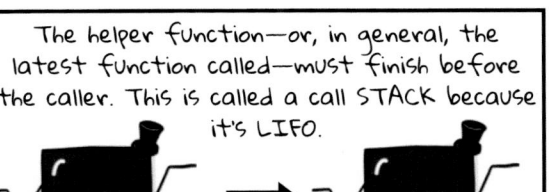

I've taken care of all cleaning up the variables!

And I return what needs to be returned!

addNums()   x + y

Think of a helper function. When we call it, we can draw another function on C. Stack.

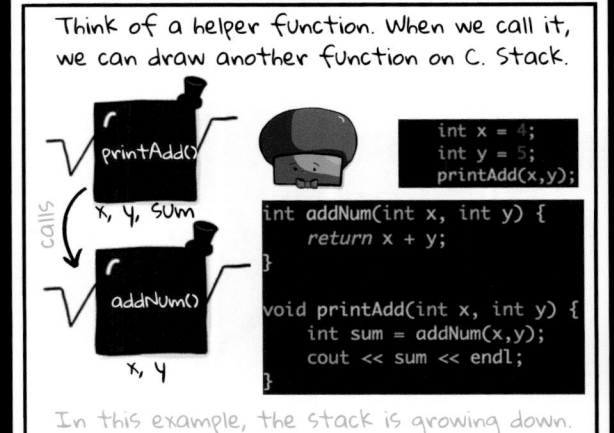

printAdd()

calls

x, y, sum

addNum()

x, y

```
int x = 4;
int y = 5;
printAdd(x,y);

int addNum(int x, int y) {
    return x + y;
}

void printAdd(int x, int y) {
    int sum = addNum(x,y);
    cout << sum << endl;
}
```

In this example, the stack is growing down.

Meet the C. Stack!
Your neighborhood friendly local, constantly stacked with a fresh batch of functions.

Not to be confused with stacks

The helper function—or, in general, the latest function called—must finish before the caller. This is called a call STACK because it's LIFO.

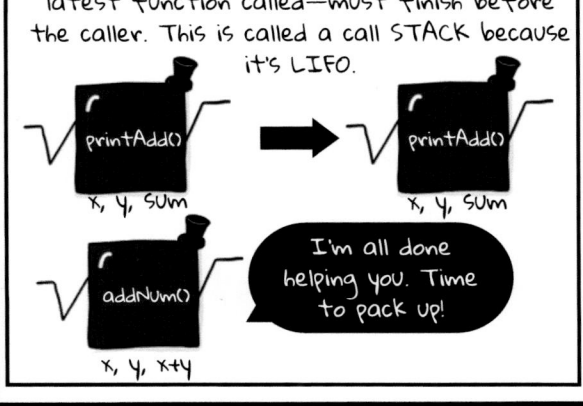

printAdd()

x, y, sum

addNum()

x, y, x+y

printAdd()

x, y, sum

I'm all done helping you. Time to pack up!

If any variables are passed in by reference, then that stack frame doesn't have any new copies of that variable.

printAdd()

x, y, sum

addNum()

```
int x = 4;
int y = 5;
printAdd(x,y);

int addNum(int& x, int& y) {
    return x + y;
}

void printAdd(int x, int y) {
    int sum = addNum(x,y);
    cout << sum << endl;
}
```

No new variables created!

Any guesses for what the first function on C. Stack usually is?

It's actually main! Each function we call after main is added until it ends and then main returns 0.

Did someone say main?

Returning 0 signifies that things have been successfully executed.

What if we want more control over our memory? For that, there's a very flexible, but dangerous, place called the heap.

Although it's nice to have C. Stack who cleans up automatically after us, HEAP allows us to manage our own memory during runtime.

I am a great power that comes with a great responsibility...

This allocation during runtime is called dynamic allocation!

But there's one caveat—we have to do the garbage collection ourselves.

YOU are responsible for cleaning ME up! You can do your own garbage collection!

To create memory on the heap, we can use the new keyword. He delivers the address of the new memory that has been created.

Here's your new address for that memory you asked for!

`new int;`

♦ **Meet HEAP!**
Where memory is made for a runtime...until we clean it up

We can then store this address of new memory in a pointer. So now the POINTER points to the heap stuff that's just been created—in this case, an int.

```
int* intPtr = new int;
```

0x123 Heap Ave.

intPtr

We can also ask for a contiguous chunk, or array of memory of a specified size. In this case, the pointer just points to the first element.

```
int* intArr = new int[3];
```

0x456 Heap Ave.

Note that here, when we are asking for memory, it is the SIZE and not the index.

To access these memory values, we can use a pointer and bracket notation to edit the actual value from the pointer.

```
//changes third arr value
intArr[2] = 5;
```

0x456 Heap Ave.

intArr

To delete an element, we use the delete keyword on its POINTER. Note that the pointer does NOT get deleted.

I've deleted the memory you were pointing to, as requested!

```
delete intPtr;
//deletes the ARRAY
delete [] intArr;
```

intPtr   intArr

Be careful to NOT dereference the pointer immediately after using delete.

Stone Mason Struct is a self-defined variable type made up of a bunch of fields stuck together. He can be useful for storing packages of things like RGB values!

Once we make him, we can use him as our own custom variable type!

```
struct Coordinate {
    int x;
    int y;
};
Coordinate origin;
```

You can call me like any other variable type!

Once he's declared, we can then access and edit those fields with the dot (.) notation.

```
origin.x = 0;
origin.y = 0;
```

The variable is really just a container for its fields and represents that collection.

I am nothing without my fields.

```
Coordinate coord;
coord.x = 3;
coord.y = 4;
```

Stone Mason Struct
Throwing stones together to make something new

Often, we'll be dealing with structs from their pointers as they can be quite large...

```
Coordinate* coordPtr = &(coord);
```

Accessing a field from a pointer involves two steps. First, we dereference the struct and second, we access the struct's field.

```
(*coordPtr).x = 1;
```

That's a lot of symbols!

The '*' gets the struct from its pointer; the '.' gets the field value from the struct.

Luckily, there exists a shorthand to access STRUCT FIELDS from a struct POINTER. This shorthand uses arrow notation (->).

```
//we're editing the struct from the pointer
coordPtr->x = 2;
coordPtr->y = 3;
```

The pointer can REACH in and grab the value.

We'll be seeing a lot of the -> symbol later on with linked data types!

We are structs that like to party on the heap! Catch ya later in chapter 6!

A SUMMARY OF SYMBOLS

	USAGE	PURPOSE
*	int* intPtr	declare a variable that's a pointer
	*(intPtr)	dereference a pointer (retrieve the value it points at)
&	&(myInt)	access a variable's memory address
	int& intArr	pass a variable in by reference
[]	intArrPtr[index]	access an element of an array pointed to on the heap
•	myStruct.field	access the field of a struct (from the struct itself)
->	myStructPtr->field Shorthand for *(myStructPtr).field	access the field of a struct from a struct pointer

Chapter Five
GETTING CLASSY
Exploring Classes in C++

Classy Class

Kemi the Client

Queen Header

Sir Cpp File

Classes in C++ allow us (the USER) to define a NEW kind of data type for other people (the CLIENT) to use.

Us Stanford ADTs are classes! We're the reason you don't know what an iterator is!

Laughs in CS106L

But how does a client of the class know how to use these new data types? How do we (the user) even begin to define our new class?

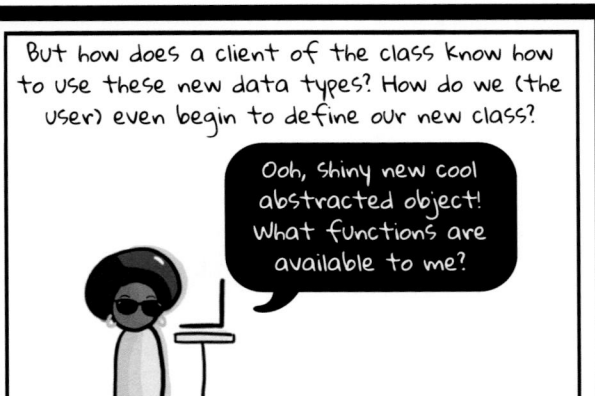
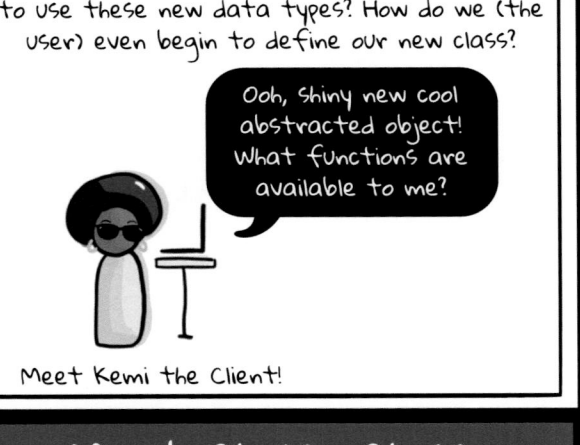

Ooh, shiny new cool abstracted object! What functions are available to me?

Meet Kemi the Client!

That's what Classy Class is here to help us explain :)

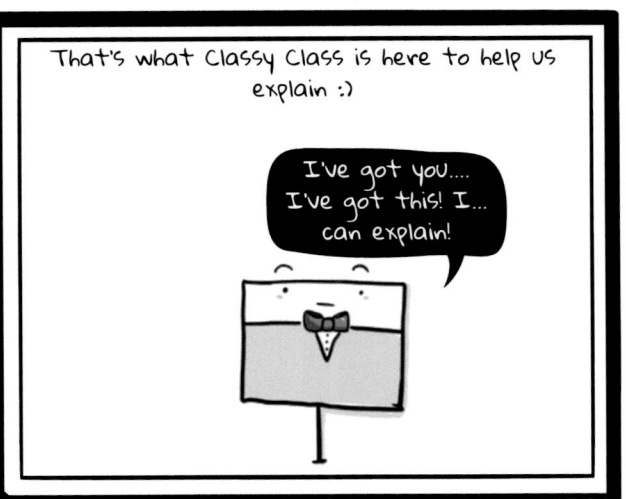

I've got you.... I've got this! I... can explain!

Within a class, everything is centered around a specific object. After creation, the client can create an instance of the class just like how we create a new variable.

```
// Form: ClassName varName
Queue<int> myQueue;
```

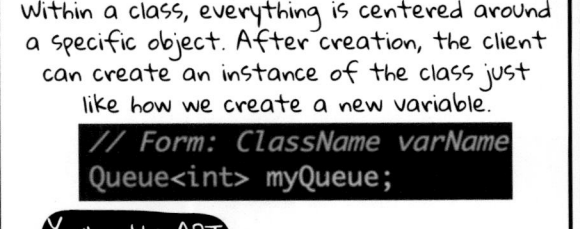

You're the ADT of my eye!

Awww shucks :)

Meet Classy Class
Giving lessons on how to use a whole new data type

Classes are very extensive and have "secret" elements that only the programmer can access.

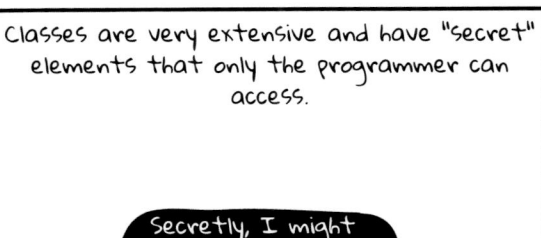

Secretly, I might be a bunch of Vectrains. Sad, I know. Alas!

These secret elements exist because under the hood, things like queues and stacks are often implemented with arrays. But why is this necessary?

I'm just an array with some circles over it and restrictions imposed ;-;

Besides the primitive types, we essentially have to build every other data type from the ground up. Luckily, there are other classes and libraries that do this for us :) .

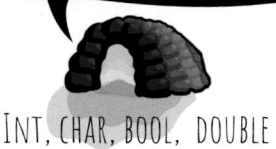

REMEMBER US...? WE ARE THE ONLY BUILT-IN FEATURES OF C++. EVERYTHING ELSE IS ABSTRACTED FROM US!

Int, char, bool, double

Using class functions is what allows the whole object.function() format.

```
//function that retrieves the number of rows
int rows = myGrid.numRows();
```

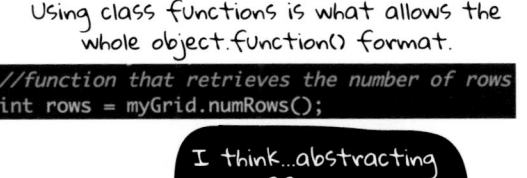
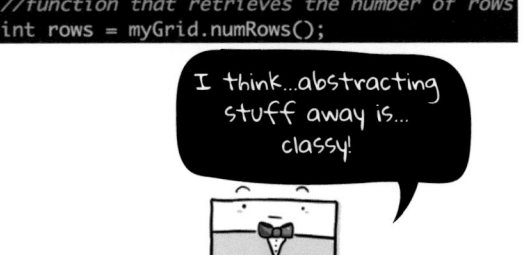

I think...abstracting stuff away is... classy!

In creating a class, we have to first decide what our central object is. Are we implementing a Queue? A Priority Queue? A Stack? A Grid?

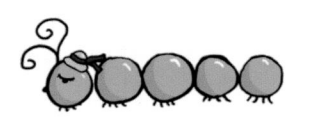

We also have to figure out what we would want and expect our CLIENT to be able to use and CALL. For example, with a queue, a client would expect to enqueue and dequeue.

If you can't enqueue and dequeue a queue, then what does that queue even do?

These are called PUBLIC member functions and variables. The client can CALL these functions but can't see their implementation.

Alas, I am blocked by a layer of abstraction!

```
Queue<int> myQueue = {1, 2, 3};
myQueue.dequeue();
```

In a queue, we can call q.dequeue() despite not seeing the underlying implementation

Defining these PUBLIC member functions and variables defines a suite of functions that the client call with the whole object.function() syntax.

```
Stack<int> myStack = {1, 2, 3};
myStack.pop();
```

Classy Class
Now presenting... an overview

But under the hood, there are some elements we need to help create PUBLIC functions. However, we don't want the client to access them.

What do you mean, I don't have access to the Queue's index?

Umm...Some things must be kept private!

Kemi can't access the underlying arrays.

These are PRIVATE member functions and variables. We implement these in order to make the public functions work.

I have a lot more depth than what you see in Cpp, Kemi..

I believe ya!

One more thing about ALL class functions, public or private—they're telepathic! Once you declare a class function or variable, it has access to ALL OTHER class elements.

NEW POWERS!

In order to define a class—the object, variables, functions—we have two types of files: a .h (header) and a .cpp file.

.h: I present all that's available publicly and privately

.cpp: I flesh all these functions out!

1

Now let's look at the .h file or header file, the HEAD of the class. She defines ALL class functions and variables, public and private.

> I'm a pretty powerful gal! To make a class function, you'll have to go through me!

Without this definition, we can't use functions/variables as members of our class.

Remember that class functions are TELEPATHIC—they simply have access to all member functions, private and public.

> I hereby grant to you all the powers that come with class membership.

> Fabulous! Now we can use variables without passing them in and also functions!

We structure .h files with public member elements followed by private ones. It has all the function prototypes and variable declarations.

> I am large, I contain multitudes.

Remember: The CLIENT can use ALL public class elements. PRIVATE elements like enlarge functions help us to implement the class but should not be exposed to the client.

> Abstraction is truly amazing.

> A classy man indeed!

> Agreed, your majesty.

Classy Class
Now presenting... header files

We define functions and variables by writing out their prototypes with extensive, general comments that allow one to quickly look at the description and understand its purpose.

> I demand long descriptive commentary such that my clients and users TRULY understand what's going on.

The constructor and destructor are two necessary public functions, which define rules for creation and destruction of our object.

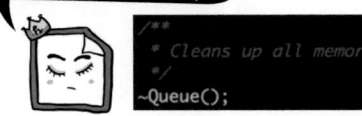

```
class Queue {
        public:
                        /**
                         * Creates a new queue.
                         */
                        Queue();
```

> Upon birth, initialize the secret array and its size. Upon death, delete the array!

```
                        /**
                         * Cleans up all memory from queue.
                         */
                        ~Queue();
```

These special functions are AUTOMATICALLY called when a class object gets created or goes out of scope.

```
void printQueue() {
    Queue<int> myQueue; //calls constructor
    myQueue.enqueue(1);
    cout << myQueue << endl;
} //calls destructor after function is out of scope
```

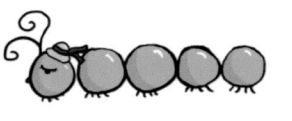

This creates an instance of the class object.

We eventually import .h to .cpp file, where these functions will be fleshed out in full.

> Royalty incoming!!

> At your liege, my Queen!

Most times, you'll find .h in a separate folder along with the other headers.

The .cpp file is where Sir Cpp has us flesh out the code for ALL our class functions. Remember that class functions are TELEPATHIC.

> I do much for our classes so Queen Header only has to head it.

Sir Cpp has some interesting syntax for our functions, though. In front of our functions, we have to indicate they are part of the class.

```
PQHeap::PQHeap() { // constructor
void PQHeap::enqueue(int elem) {
```

The notation std::string indicates that strings are in the C++ standard library.

This is because we have to let C++ know that these functions are coming from our imported class from the .h file.

> Thanks for letting me know where these functions are coming from!

We don't see std:: a lot because we are using namespace std!

Functions are declared and fleshed out in full with comments as we'd normally see, geared toward explaining the implementation side, defining parameters and return values.

```
/* This function creates an instance of a PQHeap
 * with an initial capacity of 16 .
 */
PQHeap::PQHeap() { //this is the constructor
}
```

> Detail is marvelous!

Classy Class
Now presenting... Sir Cpp

One common thing is to write the rules of creation and deletion with our constructor and destructor. This often involves the heap!

> What happens when a variable is born? When it ceases to exist?

Another common thing we'll do is initialize an underlying array to one size, only to double it as it gets full.

> Continuous, dynamic adaptation is the name of the game!

Often, you're working on the header and cpp file together, adding all functions initially in the header, fleshing them out in the .cpp, and adding functions in the header as necessary.

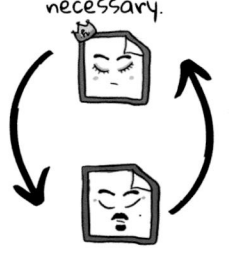

Once we are done fleshing out things in the .cpp file, we can export them for the client to use.

> Yay!

Kemi is happy!

Chapter Six
LET'S LINK UP
Linked Data Structures

The Linked List Party   Mother Treesia

Meet the Linked List Party—a data type that likes to have fun on the HEAP, one element at a time.

> Welcome to the party!

Linked Lists are chains of nodes. Each node stores some data about itself and where to find (i.e., the pointer to) the next node.

> I store data about me, myself, and I :)
> I also point to the person I love!

Within the code, they are represented by a struct like this! The data stored is usually an int, character, or string.

```
struct ListNode {
    int data;
    ListNode* next;
}
```

> Stone mason struct strikes back!

```
ListNode* topHat = new ListNode;
ListNode* headphone = new ListNode;
topHat->data = 21;
topHat->next = headphone;
```

The second field is a pointer to the next node in the PARTY! It is a STRUCT pointer to the WHOLE next node (data and all) and a bit recursive.

> Aww, you love me?

> Yes, I do :)

```
topHat->next = headphone;
```

Meet the Linked-List Party
It's a party on the heap!

If the value of NEXT is nullptr, that means it's the last node in the list.

> I love nobody....

> No party here...

```
front = nullptr;
```

```
bow->next = nullptr;
```

Since we're dealing with pointers to structs and not the structs themselves, we deal with the ->. This allows us to edit struct values from the pointer.

```
headphone = topHat->next;
int topHatData = topHat->data;
```

Remember how . and -> are different?

Note that a node's POINTER is how we access it. However, this pointer is contained in the PREVIOUS node's struct.

```
headphone = topHat->next;
int topHatData = topHat->data;
cout << headphone; //prints headphone's address
cout << topHatData; //prints 21
```

Now we can get headphone->data too!

The party is represented by a POINTER to the first node (which must be accounted for at all times). If the house is null, that means the whole linked list is empty.

> I point to the par-tay! I am how you gain access.

This pointer points to the first element and is often called list, top, or front.

We don't deal with the node struct itself as a variable.

Rather, we deal with a POINTER to that node struct.

This pointer allows us to edit the struct's data and next fields with the -> notation.

Thus, the pointer to an element comes from the PREVIOUS element's next.

Remember, SEGFAULTS often happen when we DEREFERENCE a NULLptr. This means we need to check ANYTHING we use -> with.

At times, this means checking if curr->next != null ptr, as you may be accessing curr->next->next or curr->next->data.

One of the things that can be very confusing about Linked Lists is the infamous next parameter.

There's actually a very beautiful mapping between diagram and struct fields.

INSTRUCTIONS:
Follow the arrows to the current person. From there, look at the person's data and Shirt to know the next and data value.

front	-> next	-> next	-> next	-> next
front	front->next	front->next->next	front->next->next ->next	front->next->next ->next->next
points to top hat	points to headset	points to party hat	points to bow	points to NULL
	front->data	front->next->data	front->next-> next->data	front->next->next ->next->data
	top hat data	headphone data	party hat data	bow data
firstElem = front	secElem = firstElem->next	thirdElem = secElem->next	fourthElem = thirdElem->next	lastElem = fourthElem->next

This does NOT mean that front is the first element; it means that front POINTS TO the first element.

```
void printLinkedList(ListNode* front) {
    ListNode* curr = front; //keep track of front node
    while (curr != nullptr) { //while we don't have null
        cout << curr->data; //get the current data
        curr = curr->next; //get the next node (pointer)
    }
}
```

What looping through looks like!

STEP 0: KNOW WHAT WILL CHANGE

Heads up! New party person coming here!

...AND THE IMPORTANT PEOPLE (VIPS)

before   after

toInsert

```
ListNode* beforeInsert = front->next;
ListNode* afterInsert = beforeInsert->next;
```

STEP 1: MAKE THE NEW ELEMENT POINT TO THE NEXT ELEMENT

My love for you was... inevitable!

```
toInsert->next = afterInsert;
```

STEP 2: MAKE THE PREVIOUS ELEMENT POINT TO THE NEW ELEMENT

Man, I've got to learn to love again!

```
beforeInsert->next = toInsert;
```

The Linked-List Party
Exploring one way to add people to the party

DONE!

Thanks for fully integrating me!

No changes, just rearranged graphically

What steps would change if we prepended the new element (inserted it at the front)?

When MY shirt changes, pass me in by reference ;)

What steps would change if we appended the new element (inserted at the back)?

Hullo!

Some Questions

What would change if we swapped step 1 and step 2? Would the number of steps change?

Is prepending or appending more efficient? What is the Big-O of each? HINT: one of these has a Big-O of O(1)!

If we prepend in a separate function, what additional consideration would we have to make when defining our function parameters?

STEP 0: KNOW WHAT WILL CHANGE

I finally get integrated only to be kicked back out?! Shame.

...AND THE IMPORTANT LINKS

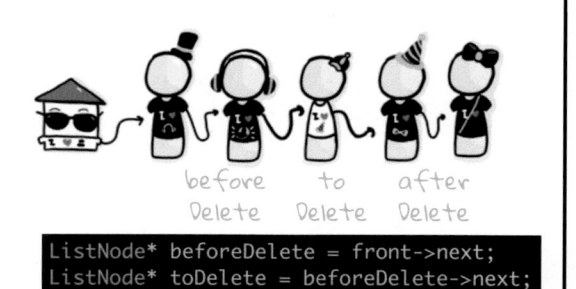

before Delete   to Delete   after Delete

```
ListNode* beforeDelete = front->next;
ListNode* toDelete = beforeDelete->next;
ListNode* afterDelete = toDelete->next;
```

STEP 1: FIND AND STORE POINTER FOR ELEMENT TO BE DELETED

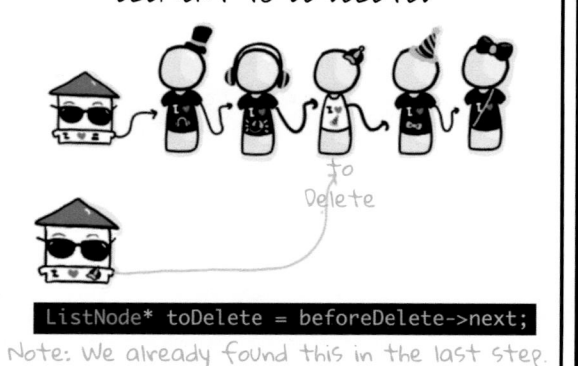

to Delete

```
ListNode* toDelete = beforeDelete->next;
```

Note: We already found this in the last step.

STEP 2: REWIRE THE ELEMENT BEFORE TO POINT TO ELEMENT AFTER

```
beforeDelete->next = afterDelete;
```

The Linked-List Party
Exploring one way to remove people from the party

STEP 3: DELETE ELEMENT and DONE!

```
delete toDelete;
```

What steps would change if we removed from the front?

What steps would change if we removed from the back?

Some Questions

Why can't we just delete the element right from the start?

When we set two pointers equal to each other, what happens?

Is back removal or front removal more efficient? What is the Big-O of each?

Meet another Linked Data Structure— Mother Treesia! She's a tree, a structure that is parent to some number of "children" trees or none at all.

They say I'm a cool mom.

In this class, we deal with BINARY trees, trees that have at most two children trees.

A tree is made of nodes. The top one is called the root. Nodes with no children are leaves. All nodes have AT MOST one parent. No cycles are allowed.

We're leaves! We've got no children!

I am root.

In code, trees are represented by structs like this. The first field has data about the tree itself, exactly like Linked Lists.

```
struct TreeNode {
    string data; //can be any type
    TreeNode* left;
    TreeNode* right;
};

root->data = "Tippity Top";
```

I store some stuff about myself too!

The other fields represent the left and right children. This is analogous to the next field with Linked Lists, but instead of one node, there are two!

```
TreeNode* leftChild = root->left;
TreeNode* rightChild = root->right;
```

You can use me to get to my children!

Mother Treesia
A calm, cool collection

If there isn't a child, then the left or right field is nullptr. If both children are null, then the node is a leaf node.

```
if (leftChild->left == nullptr) {
    if (leftChild->right == nullptr) {
        cout << "LEAF!!!" << endl;
    }
}
```

A TreeNode* will point to the top of the tree structure, often called root. This is analogous to front in a Linked List. Mother Treesia also sits on the heap.

I merely point to the first node.

`TreeNode* root` ☆

Since these children are ALSO trees, the tree structure lends itself to much recursion!

Self-similarity, yay!

I'm a child but also a parent!

There is a special kind of tree called a binary search tree. All elements left of any node are less than it; all elements right of it are greater. It can be searched in O(log n)!

ALGORITHMS

ILLUSTRATED

In this latest edition:
BINARY SEARCH TREES

Getting the BST of both worlds.

Binary search is a cool algorithm that takes $O(\log n)$.

By definition, our search is halved every time! Instead of going through all of the elements, we are GUARANTEED we will be only searching through half of them!

Learn about the algorithm that has Big-O smiling!

The Tree Traversals

Sometimes we will want to do a task (like printing) on each node of the tree. But how might we go about reaching every single node? Since each child of a tree is also a tree, we can recursively traverse! In class, we cover three main tree traversals: pre-order, in-order, and post-order.

Let's look at how we might print the tree in each one of these orders!

Pre

"Me and then my children"

This is useful for things like creation where the parent needs to go first.

Once the parent goes, we can recursively do the children, where each child then becomes a parent and procreates.

```
void printPre(TreeNode* root) {
    if (root == nullptr) {
        return;
    }
    cout << root->data;
    printTreePre(root->left);
    printTreePre(root->right);
}
```

In

"In order, from left to right"

We can do this traversal by going left to right with a pencil and seeing which nodes we hit first.

. With binary search trees, the tree gets sorted in order and search takes O(log n)!

```
void printIn(TreeNode* root) {
    if (root == nullptr) {
        return;
    }
    printTreeIn(root->left);
    cout << root->data;
    printTreeIn(root->right);
}
```

Post

"My children go before me"

Although this seems selfless, this is most useful for things like deletion!

This is because we need to delete all the children first lest we have a memory leak from an abandoned child!

```
void printPost(TreeNode* root) {
    if (root == nullptr) {
        return;
    }
    printTreePost(root->left);
    printTreePost(root->right);
    cout << root->data;
}
```

Each traversal is defined by the PLACEMENT of the parent. The left child always goes into its RECURSIVE call before the right. And the BASE CASE is when the root is nullptr. We must ALWAYS check for this, as accessing any child involves dereferencing a pointer!

It's just by convention my lil' sib!

Why do you always get to go first?

The Tree Traversals

So how can tree traversals cover the whole tree if they only touch upon the left and right children?

Remember that the left child is also a whole tree. When we go into its recursive function, the left child becomes a parent. Soon after, its left child becomes a parent in its recursive call, and so on and so forth. When we hit a leaf, both of its children are null, quickly hitting the base case and returning back up to finish execution. This means that LEAF nodes will ALWAYS be the first to finish their entire function. The left and right children aren't finished until their whole tree is! Only when both children are done executing do the left or right helper recursive functions finish.

Given the following trees, what would be the result of traversing in pre, in, and post order?

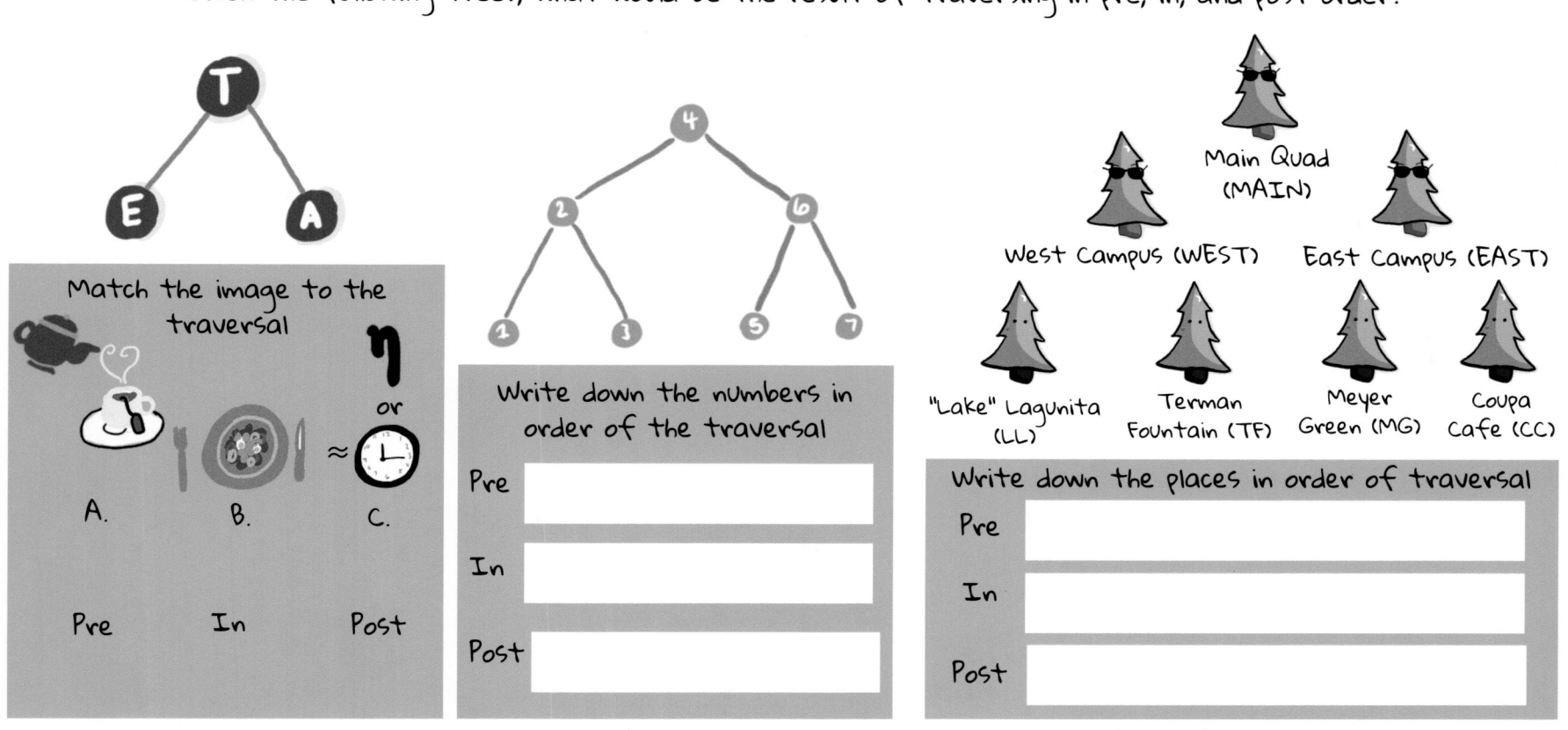

Match the image to the traversal

A.　　　B.　　　C.

≈　η or ◷

Pre　　In　　Post

Write down the numbers in order of the traversal

Pre

In

Post

Main Quad (MAIN)

West Campus (WEST)　　East Campus (EAST)

"Lake" Lagunita (LL)　　Terman Fountain (TF)　　Meyer Green (MG)　　Coupa Cafe (CC)

Write down the places in order of traversal

Pre

In

Post

ANSWERS: PRE-ORDER: A (TEA); 4213657; MAIN, WEST, LL, TF, EAST, MG, CC.
IN-ORDER: C (ETA); 1234567; LL, WEST, TF, MAIN, MG, EAST, CC.
POST-ORDER: B (EAT); 1325764; LL, TF, WEST, MG, CC, EAST, MAIN.

3

CS106B

You got through the CS106B side of the comic

(or you are a very curious cat)!

Let's look back at the ADVENTURE

or if you're peeking, what's in store :)!

START

We started with orienting ourselves in the C++ language.

After, we dove into the complex yet curious world of ADTs.

Then linked everything together with some new structs, ending in Stanford fashion with trees!

We then got classy with classes, jumping into the essence of OOP.

We then went over some of the coolest of the coolest of the coolest of concepts, learning about efficiency and recursion!

And we expanded our horizons, exploring and experimenting with computer memory and storage.

FINISH

C O N G R A T S